DIVINE DIRECTIONS

HOW GOD GUIDES YOUR PATH

Divine Directions presents a master class in beautiful storytelling. Sharla Fritz expertly weaves journeys of familiar biblical characters with her own experiences to present fresh insights into God's guiding hand throughout our lives. The stories felt like a personal invitation to reflect on my own spiritual journey. To notice God's faithful hand through my muddy valleys and snow-capped highs. I laughed out loud and felt tears of thankfulness spill over as God used this book to renew my spirit. If you need a spiritual jump-start, *Divine Directions* is sweeter than honey.

—Donna Snow, founder of Artesian Ministries and author of *Strong and Courageous: Studying God's Promises in Joshua*

Sharla navigates Scripture, history, and the theme of spiritual journeys with deep perception and fresh perspective. I found myself lingering over the surprising insights that she shared, wanting to tuck them in my heart to remember in my own life travels. This study is so rich and applicable to everyday life that I can see ladies pouring over it and having rich and meaningful discussion together as they dig into God's Word, especially the testimonies of those who have walked before us. I'm certain that Sharla's thoughtful work will bless and encourage you on your faith journey!

— Lindsay Hausch, Christian author and speaker

Reading Sharla Fritz's most recent Bible study, *Divine Directions: How God Guides Your Path*, I knew I was in good hands. Sharla frames each chapter by relating stories of her own journeying before setting eight familiar biblical figures in historical time, place, and circumstance. What decisions did they make? How did they navigate the uncertainties in their lives? How do we? Sharla guides and challenges her readers to connect and reflect, to dig into the Word, to learn more about how God leads us on our life journeys. This is a compelling study for anyone—in individual or group settings—seeking to grow in faith.

— Carole Duff, author of *Wisdom Builds Her House*

With the wisdom of a lifelong traveler in the way of Jesus, Sharla Fritz weaves her words together with one goal in mind: to help others find their way in life as they find their way with Jesus.

With humor, imagination, careful exposition of the Bible, and well-crafted questions for personal or group study, Sharla shows us how God guided men and women ages ago. She also gently reminds us that this same God really does still guide those who seek Him.

— Afton Rorvik, author of *Storm Sisters: Friends Through All Seasons* and *Living Connected: An Introvert's Guide to Friendship*

DIVINE DIRECTIONS

HOW GOD GUIDES YOUR PATH

Sharla Fritz

CONCORDIA PUBLISHING HOUSE • SAINT LOUIS

Dedication

To my father, who instilled in me a love of travel and adventure.

Published by Concordia Publishing House
3558 S. Jefferson Ave., St. Louis, MO 63118-3968
1-800-325-3040 · cph.org

Library of Congress Cataloging-in-Publication Data

Names: Fritz, Sharla, author.

Title: Divine destinations : how God plans your path / Sharla Fritz.

Description: Saint Louis : Concordia Publishing House, [2025] | Includes bibliographical references. | Summary: "Through an examination of eight journeys in the Bible, this women's Bible study will show readers how God guides us through the mountains and valleys of life through His Word and constant presence. This Bible study will include discussion questions, answers, maps, and other features"-- Provided by publisher.

Identifiers: LCCN 2024054341 (print) | LCCN 2024054342 (ebook) | ISBN 9780758677976 (paperback) | ISBN 9780758677983 (ebook)

Subjects: LCSH: Bible--Biography--Study and teaching. | Christian life--Biblical teaching.

Classification: LCC BS605.3 .F75 2025 (print) | LCC BS605.3 (ebook) | DDC 248.4--dc23/eng/20250215

LC record available at https://lccn.loc.gov/2024054341

LC ebook record available at https://lccn.loc.gov/2024054342

Manufactured in the United States of America

1 2 3 4 5 6 7 8 9 10 34 33 32 31 30 29 28 27 26 25

Contents

INTRODUCTION

Misty fjords. Blue ice glaciers. Stunning snow-capped mountains reflected in crystal clear waters.

My husband and I observed all these sights on an Alaskan cruise. Every stop on our journey brought new delights as we experienced a corner of God's creation we had never seen before. Every port gave us new reasons to ooh and aah over picturesque wonders.

Not only did we enjoy the views but we reveled in the accommodations of our mode of transportation. Due to our limited funds, we had booked an inner cabin, which meant we could conveniently access the closet without even getting out of bed! But it was still the most luxurious trip we had ever taken. We could eat whenever we wanted and pick from an extensive menu. We could watch a magic show or participate in an exercise class. We could find entertainment in the theater or in a cooking demonstration. We could sit and listen to a guitarist or find a comfortable chair and simply watch the spectacular scenery glide by.

Don't you wish life was like a cruise? Wouldn't it be awesome to choose your favorite destination and itinerary, and then move through life gliding from one magnificent port to the next? Travel in comfort along the way, having all your needs and desires met?

Our life journeys, however, rarely resemble a scenic cruise. Instead of floating on a calm sea in a luxury sailing vessel, our voyages may feel like a sinking ship during a storm. Or life resembles a hike through a dark and bewildering forest without a map. Or the journey seems like a trek through a bleak wilderness with stops in locations we would never willingly choose.

When our journeys seem arduous and confusing, we wonder how we can find a smoother way. We ask questions like these: "Should I pursue this degree? Take this job? Buy this house? Retire? Move to a different city?" We want guidance and direction. We yearn for God to give us a map that clearly points out the roads and pathways He wants us to take.

While God rarely provides us with such a detailed map for our choices, He does provide guidance in His Word for our life. The Bible is filled with accounts of journeys that can help us decide the best path forward in our own life. Abraham traveled from Ur to Canaan. Hagar traveled into the wilderness and back. Rebekah took a path to a new life far from home. Moses led the people of Israel from Egypt to the border of the Promised Land. Ruth left her home in Moab and went with her mother-in-law, Naomi, to a new country. Jonah made his journey longer by heading in the opposite direction before obeying God's instructions. The Magi followed a sign in the sky to find the King. Paul journeyed all over the known world to share the Gospel. As we examine these stories in this Bible study, we will glean scriptural principles that will direct our own treks through life. By looking at these journeys, we will learn God's divine directions and His plan for our paths.

USING THIS BOOK

In *Divine Directions: How God Guides Your Path*, you will closely examine eight journeys God's people took in the Bible. Long journeys through deserts and voyages across seas. Excursions to the unknown and trips to a new life. Adventures led by a star and escorted by a cloud. Routes begun in rebellion and travels launched in hope.

As you study these journeys, you will learn about their significance in the story of God's people and the historical context of that account. You will see how each expedition informs your own path. You will learn how God guided His people in the past. And you will explore how He still leads us today.

You may choose to study the concepts of God's guidance by reading straight through the chapters. Each chapter includes the following:

- a **timeline** to help you see how that particular person's life fits in history
- a **map** to give geographical perspective of where he or she lived
- **historical information** about the time and place being studied to help you envision how each Bible character lived

In addition to reading the chapters in this book, I hope you will go deeper into the Word by engaging in the Bible study questions in the back of the book, beginning on page 151. There you will find four sections to help you: "Reflect on the Reading," "Dig into the Word," "God's Word Is the Map to Your Life," and "Create a Project."

I encourage you to invite a few others to join you as you examine these biblical journeys. Share your own stories and encourage others to share theirs. This study is designed to be completed in eight weeks, but if your meeting time is short or if you want to take the journey at a slower pace, the study is adaptable and you can take two weeks for every chapter. In that case, you could do the reading and the "Reflect on the Reading" questions in the back of the book one week. Then complete the "Dig into the Word," "God's Word Is the Map to Your Life," and "Create a Project" sections the next week.

As you study, do the following:

- Begin each chapter with prayer.
- Rely on Scripture to guide your discussions.
- Keep what is said in your group confidential, unless you are given permission to share information outside the group.

May the Lord bless you as you rejoice in God's guiding hand.

CHAPTER 1

ABRAM

A Trek to Canaan

TIMELINE

Abram (Abraham) .... 2100 BC

The world whizzed by as we drove west through Wisconsin, Minnesota, South Dakota, and Wyoming. Summer brought long hours of sunlight to the expanses of farmland, but that sun baked the interior of our little red Nissan Sentra. The wind coming through the windows wasn't enough to cool us, so I sometimes resorted to dropping ice down the back of my shirt to lower my body temperature.

We were driving to Missoula, Montana, in our just-purchased little red car. And because we were moving to a northern state, we thought we wouldn't need air conditioning. Who would have thought that temperatures would reach 102 degrees on the very day we reached our destination.

But we had more complications than a three-day, cross-country drive in a car without air conditioning. When my husband, John, had graduated from Concordia Seminary, St. Louis, a few months earlier, we never expected that his first call would be to a church in Montana! He had requested to serve at a church in the northeastern part of the United States, and according to every geography lesson I'd ever had, Montana did not qualify.

I clearly remember the night of the call service at the seminary, when all of the graduates learned the locations of their first assignments. In my mind's eye, I still see my husband walking to the front of the chapel. When the seminary official said, "John Fritz—First Lutheran Church, Missoula, Montana," his face drained of all color.

After the service, we looked at the information about the church in a state of shock. Some of John's classmates gleefully read about their new churches and homes, but we stood with furrowed brows and mouths agape.

Of course, there were other students who also questioned where the seminary had placed them. Even though everyone had theoretically accepted the idea that the call process expressed God's will on their lives, when the call had instructed someone to go in the opposite direction of where that person wanted to go, it was easy to say, "God couldn't want me to go there." In fact, a couple of John's classmates declined their calls and chose to wait for something different.

We were tempted to do the same. "Missoula, Montana? Are You sure, Lord? We don't know anyone there. How can we go so far from our families in Wisconsin?" Having never been to Montana, we thought that if it wasn't the end of the world, we could certainly see it from there.

Several people encouraged John to reject the call. But we had prayed God would guide the call process and give us direction. Now all those prayers resulted in a call to Montana. Would we accept God's plan and obey Him?

We did. And that's how we ended up making the three-day, cross-country trip from Wausau, Wisconsin, where both of our parents lived, to our new home 1,400 miles away. I just wish we had sprung for air conditioning!

MAP © CONCORDIA PUBLISHING HOUSE

SETTING THE SCENE

The patriarch Abraham also took a long, cross-country expedition. When we first met him in Genesis 12, he was still named Abram, and God had called him to leave his home and everything he knew. This sounds a little like my journey with my husband, but at least we knew our destination. God didn't provide that much information to Abram. The Lord simply said, "Go" (v. 1).

Born around 2000 BC, Abram lived in the Sumerian city of Ur. An important port city near the Persian Gulf with a population of two hundred thousand to three hundred thousand, its residents enjoyed a comfortable life. Middle-class families lived in homes with ten to twenty rooms and had plenty of food and opportunities for education.[1]

The people of the city worshiped many gods, including Sin, a popular moon god. So how did Abram come to know Yahweh in a land of idols? How did he hear the true God's call when everyone else called out to a moon god? The Bible doesn't give us those details, just like God didn't give Abram details about his destination. He just said, "Go from your country and your kindred and your father's house to the land that I will show you" (v. 1).

I don't know about you, but when I travel, I like to have my itinerary planned, routes identified, and hotels booked. Abram had none of that. God asked him to step out in faith—to go. The Lord would provide details along the way. Although Abram didn't have a AAA itinerary mapped out for him, we know that the first nine hundred miles of his trip took him west to Haran, a city in the northern region of Mesopotamia. Later, during the last leg of his journey, he traveled about five hundred miles south to Canaan.

Abram and Sarai traveled about the same distance my husband and I did—approximately 1,400 miles. But while John and I could count on rest stops that included cool drinks and hot food, Abram wouldn't have been able to find a quick cheeseburger along the way. We checked into motels with comfy beds and clean sheets ready for our weary bodies. When Abram and company stopped for the night, they had to set up their tents, make the beds, start a fire, and cook their own food. No Comfort Inns for Abram and Sarai.

THE JOURNEY

I don't know what Abram and Sarai went through because the Bible doesn't reveal many of the details, but I can imagine what it might have been like for them. I visualize Abram as he left Haran riding his camel through a dry and barren land. As he shielded his eyes from the sun, I can see him looking down the ancient path, wondering what lay ahead. He could never have pictured this life when they lived in Ur. He looked over at Sarai riding next to him and knew she also never thought they would leave their comfortable home.

FREQUENT TRAVELER MILES

Abram would have earned many travel points in his lifetime. Not only did he travel about 1,400 miles from Ur to Canaan but later journeys took him to Egypt, back to Canaan, and up to the northern city of Dan. He also spent time in Hebron, Beersheba, Gerar in the land of the Philistines, and Salem (later known as Jerusalem).

He said a silent prayer of thanksgiving for this woman who didn't abandon him when he announced that God had told them to leave. Perhaps, when he told her that God hadn't revealed their path or their destination, she thought he was as crazy as the cuckoo birds they sometimes saw near their home, but she went with him anyway.

At first, they followed the great Euphrates River so they would have access to water along the way. They made quite a sight: an old man and his wife traveling with an even older man, his father, Terah. His nephew Lot and all their servants and worldly goods completed the party.

God didn't provide a map, but He revealed which direction He wanted them to go. For a time, Abram and his family settled in the city of Haran, but that was not an ideal place to live since the people there worshiped the moon god Sin. After Terah died, God again called Abram to move.

So now they traveled south. They passed through the city of Damascus and proceeded to the land of the Canaanites. Each day, they packed up their tents and belongings. If traveling went well, they traversed about twenty miles. It's easy for us to think that Abram must have longed for the old days when he and Sarai lived in a comfortable home with familiar friends nearby. But nothing could compare to the adventure of faith he lived, trusting the true God of blessing with each step he took.

CHOOSING CONFIDENCE IN GOD OVER CLARITY OF COURSE

When my husband and I drove from Wisconsin to Montana, we had a map. (Yep, a *paper* map!) The map clearly indicated the best road to our destination: I-90 through Wisconsin, Minnesota, South Dakota, Wyoming, and Montana.

Along the way, however, we started to question the route to our new home. What made us doubt our decision to follow that highway? The lack of people! At one point in our drive through Wyoming, we saw cattle. We saw fields. But while traveling at fifty-five miles per hour, we didn't see a single vehicle or human for an entire hour. And when we finally saw a vehicle, it was a pickup truck that hauled two spare tires and a gas can. Clearly, people living in Wyoming were prepared for the wilderness.

We wondered, "Would Missoula look like this? Maybe we should just turn around." Although we had clarity of route, we didn't always have clarity of heart.

Abram, on the other hand, had clarity of heart even if he didn't have clarity of route. He had chosen to obey God's calling and set out before knowing where he would end up.

The book of Hebrews tells us,

> By faith Abraham obeyed when he was called to go out to a place that he was to receive as an inheritance. And he went out, not knowing where he was going. By faith he went to live in the land of promise, as in a foreign land, living in tents with Isaac and Jacob, heirs with him of the same promise. For he was looking forward to the city that has foundations, whose designer and builder is God. (Hebrews 11:8–10)

Let's examine this passage a little more closely.

"By faith [Abram] . . . went out, not knowing where he was going" (Hebrews 11:8). We don't know the specifics of how God guided Abram to the land of Canaan. Did God speak to Abram? Did He use other people to give him directions? I would prefer a few giant road signs along the

way that said, "Turn left here!" I imagine that the traveler from Ur would have liked a detailed map and clear signs as much as I would. But what does God desire? To build faith.

Hebrews 11:1 defines faith this way: "Now faith is the assurance of things hoped for, the conviction of things *not* seen" (emphasis added).

In other words, faith is the opposite of clarity. We all want clarity. When I searched the word *clarity* on the internet, my search engine came up with six hundred million entries on the subject. We want clarity in work, relationships, financial decisions. Can't someone just tell us the right way to go and the best thing to do?

But if we have clarity, we don't need faith. Clarity means we can already distinguish which direction to go. **Because God always desires to strengthen our faith in Him, sometimes He withholds clarity.** God didn't provide all the details of the patriarch's journey in an effort to build his faith. God assures us of our final destination in heaven, but He doesn't point out all the twists, turns, detours, avalanches, and bridge closings we'll encounter ahead of time because He wants to build our trust in Him and in His turn-by-turn directions as we need them.

"By faith he went to live in the land of promise, as in a foreign land" (Hebrews 11:9). Why did God call Abram out of Ur? Out of Haran? Genesis 12:1 tells us that God said, "Go from your *country* and your *kindred* and your *father's house* to the land that I will show you" (emphasis added).

Perhaps God called Abram away from his *country* because both Ur and Haran were centers for the moon god Sin. (What an appropriate name for a false god!) Perhaps if Abram had continued to live in those places, he would have been tempted to turn to that idol to fit in with the culture. Maybe God asked Abram to leave his *kindred* because often each family clan had its own favorite gods. Abram's relatives may have pressured Abram to worship the gods they believed in. Perhaps God asked Abram to leave his *father's house* because Terah was an idolater (see Joshua 24:2). In leaving the land of his father, Abram left behind his earthly inheritance. But God promised Abram that He would give him a new land and make him into a great nation. Even with divine direction, that promise must have seemed like an improbability since Abram left Haran at age 75 without any children.

John and I felt a bit like Abram might have while we were driving to Montana. We left the Midwest, where we had always lived, to go to a new city we had never seen. We left behind all our friends and relatives to go to a place where we knew no one. Like Abram, we experienced a trust-building exercise.

Sometimes God calls us out of the familiar into the foreign to increase our dependence on Him.

By faith, Abram went "living in tents with Isaac and Jacob. . . . He was looking forward to the city that has foundations, whose designer and builder is God" (Hebrews 11:9, 10). We know that Ur was a center of civilization where middle-class families lived in houses. Did Sarai complain when they had to give up a stable existence to live an itinerant lifestyle?

"Living in tents" meant Abram and Sarai never quite settled. But it also meant they could more easily respond to God if He instructed them to move again. "Living in tents" provides a picture of our life on earth, or at least what it should look like. Most of us long to settle in a place with a secure home with an abundance of family and friends nearby, but God may call us to live unsettled. He reminds us not to get too comfortable here on earth because this is not our permanent home. We, like Abram, can look "forward to the city that has foundations, whose designer and builder is God" (v. 10).

While we would like perfect clarity on the details and decisions of our lives, God wants to increase our confidence in Him. Finding ourselves on a road obscured by the fog of uncertainty might be the best place because that's where we turn to God, who delights in showing us His way.

REMEMBER TO PACK: HOLY INDIFFERENCE

When we travel, we need to pack our suitcases with clothes and toiletries—the necessities of life. What essentials should we pack for our life journeys?

One essential to carry on our quest to find God's will for our lives is an attitude of holy indifference. Ignatius of Loyola (1491–1556) coined the term *holy indifference* in his book *Spiritual Exercises*. While we usually view indifference as a negative, holy indifference means caring deeply about loving God and doing His will while being indifferent about where God's will leads us. This attitude means we desire the Lord's path for our life more than our own personal comfort, fame, or pleasure.*

How often have I said I want God's will, but in reality I simply want God to rubber-stamp the plans I have for my life? If I truly want God to direct my life, I need to give up my preconceived ideas about the specifics of my path. I need to pack up some holy indifference based on faith in God's goodness.

**See "Prayer of Indifference and Detachment," The Ignatian Journey (website), accessed April 24, 2024, https://www.theignatianjourney.com/prayer-of-indifference-and-detachment.*

WHEN FEAR UPENDS FAITH

When we finally arrived in Missoula, we were pleasantly surprised to find a lovely small city nestled in the Rocky Mountains. The home the church found for us to rent was situated on the side of one of those rocky mountains and had a spectacular view of the city and the surrounding peaks.

Some of my fears were relieved. We had arrived in a place filled with welcoming people and gorgeous scenery. But after I unpacked the mountain of boxes, my days felt empty. I didn't have a job. I didn't have friends. I began to fear that Missoula would never feel like home.

At times, fear may upend our faith. Fear may send us in the wrong direction. Abram demonstrated great trust in obeying God's call to embark on a journey without a specific itinerary or destination, but his faith stumbled when a famine struck the land of Canaan. Genesis 12:10 tells us, "Now there was a famine in the land. So Abram went down to Egypt to sojourn there, for the famine was severe in the land." The Bible doesn't say that God told Abram to go to Egypt, so one could argue that Abram's faith had already faltered when he journeyed to Egypt instead of staying in the land of promise and trusting God to provide for him. But God did not forbid Abram to go to Egypt (as He later did with Isaac in Genesis 26 when another famine occurred in Canaan). Logic and common sense guided Abram south to the land where crops did not depend as much on rainfall as on the annual flooding of the Nile River. But even if we cannot find fault with Abram's trust in God by his going to Egypt, what happened there demonstrated his fear rather than his faith. The account goes on:

> When he was about to enter Egypt, he said to Sarai his wife, "I know that you are a woman beautiful in appearance, and when the Egyptians see you, they will say, 'This is his wife.' Then they will kill me, but they will let you live. Say you are my sister, that it may go well with me because of you, and that my life may be spared for your sake." (Genesis 12:11–13)

You may remember Sarai was indeed Abram's half-sister—they had the same father. But Abram's request forced Sarai to lie about the true nature of their relationship. Why would he put his wife's welfare in danger like that?

Fear. Abram's fear for the preservation of his own life upended his faith in a God who could certainly have protected him from any danger, including famine in Canaan or bad guys in Egypt.

When Abram and Sarai arrived in Egypt, things played out just as Abram imagined they would. The couple entered the country, and "the Egyptians saw that the woman was very beautiful" (Genesis 12:14). They reported her beauty to Pharaoh, who immediately took her into his house. At this point in her life, Sarai would have qualified for Medicare, yet Pharaoh, the most important man in the world, desired her. (Don't you wish you knew her brand of beauty cream?)

This situation could have put God's promise for Abram's offspring and the making of a great nation in jeopardy. But, most likely, Pharaoh would have followed ancient marriage rituals that prescribed a waiting period long enough to see if the bride was pregnant by someone else.[2] And, of course, God protected Sarai. Before the situation posed a problem for the promise, God sent plagues on Pharaoh and his house. The Egyptian ruler somehow ascertained that the plagues came as a result of him taking Sarai into his house. He also somehow realized she was Abram's wife. Pharaoh confronted Abram, and then he sent Abram and Sarai away with all they had, including the people and animals he had given Abram: "sheep, oxen, male donkeys, male servants, female servants, female donkeys, and camels" (Genesis 12:16).

You might think God would have given up on Abram after such a fantastic faith failure. That He would go searching for someone who wouldn't lie to protect his own skin while putting his wife in danger. That the Lord would abandon Abram because he let fear upend his faith.

But God didn't abandon this flawed man. How reassuring that the Lord doesn't give up on His people when their faith falters! I may not have faced famine and evil rulers trying to get my spouse, but my life's journey has also had some stopovers in places I should have avoided altogether. I stayed too long in the "Why me, Lord?" places when I suffered miscarriages. I frequently visited "I Know Better, God," when my daughter and her family lived thousands of miles away in China for ten years.

So Abram's story reassures me. **God won't abandon us when fear upends our faith.** He won't give up on us when we resort to human tactics in an effort to save ourselves instead of trusting in His omnipotent power. He doesn't leave us at Exit 102 when our faith fizzles out. Instead, He gently leads us back to the road of His promise. His Spirit fills our tanks with His grace and forgiveness when our rest stop includes reading His Word and receiving the Lord's Supper.

REMEMBER TO PACK: PRAYER

Fear often threatens to upend our faith. It hides at every bend in the road, insinuating that God won't protect us, won't provide. Jesus knew the realities of Satan's enticements to abandon trust, so He taught us to pray, "And lead us not into temptation" (Matthew 6:13). To guard our hearts, let's pray, "Heavenly Father, guard and keep us from the assaults of the devil, the deception of the world, and the desires of our sinful nature. Protect us that we may not be deceived or misled by lies about You, be overcome by despair of Your mercy, or be seduced into a way of life that leads only to death. Shield us by Your grace and strengthen us by Your Word and Spirit that we may withstand every attack and finally win the victory; through Jesus Christ, our Lord. Amen."*

* *Small Catechism, Lord's Prayer, Sixth Petition, Prayer at Question 284.*

FORMABLE FAITH OVER FAULTLESS DECISIONS

After John and I arrived in Missoula, we could have continued to question our decision. We liked some aspects of living in Montana, like the great skiing and stunning scenery. But we continued to struggle with living so far from our loved ones. I'm sure you have experienced this in your own life. Every path we take has both spectacular vistas and treacherous terrain.

In our modern Western world, we have the privilege of choice. A century ago, a woman not born to wealth would have had little choice about where she lived. And someone living today in an impoverished country has few options for employment. But most of us have seemingly unlimited possibilities. At various points in our lives, we might think,

"Should I take the path to college A or the one to university B? Should I travel the path toward a career in the medical field, or would the highway to a business profession end up in a more satisfying place? Should I stay on this career road for a few more years, or should I take the exit to early retirement?"

We might even worry that taking the wrong road will lead to disappointment. The wrong highway will dead end at failure. What if no U-turns are allowed?

After Abram returned from Egypt, he faced a decision. Genesis 13:2 tells us, "Abram was very rich in livestock, in silver, and in gold." And Abram's nephew Lot, who traveled with Abram, "also had flocks and herds and tents, so that the land could not support both of them dwelling together; for their possessions were so great that they could not dwell together" (vv. 5–6). Abram's herdsmen began fighting Lot's herdsmen over grazing land. They both had so much livestock that they needed to separate.

Abram brought up the problem with Lot:

> Let there be no strife between you and me, and between your herdsmen and my herdsmen, for we are kinsmen. Is not the whole land before you? Separate yourself from me. If you take the left hand, then I will go to the right, or if you take the right hand, then I will go to the left. (vv. 8–9)

At this point, Lot should have deferred to his elder uncle Abram, who had treated him like a son. But Lot looked over at the Jordan Valley and decided it was the most favorable for his flocks and herds. Lot unabashedly took the land.

Abram now had what seemed like second-rate property. If it were me, I doubt I would have given someone else the first choice. I probably would have opted to keep the best for myself. But we can surmise that

Abram had learned that he could trust God to protect him and care for him. That his safety and prosperity didn't depend on his own actions but on God's blessing. He didn't fret about getting the best land or if he went to the right or to the left because God had promised to bless him. Abram had seen how God had protected and provided for him even when he had majorly messed up, so he could count on God's blessing again.

This attitude would serve us well in the decisions we need to make, particularly decisions that are nonmoral. God's commandments for life don't include "Thou shalt buy a house in Nome, Alaska," or "Thou shalt not become an engineer." In nonmoral decisions, our options can be God-pleasing if we keep God's number one commandment in mind: "Love the Lord your God with all your heart and with all your soul and with all your mind" (Matthew 22:37).

Many people agonize over decisions, fearing that taking the wrong road will ruin the rest of their lives. High school students may stay awake at night wondering if not getting into the top school will mean a meaningless career in a mediocre city with a minimal salary. Young singles stress out over finding their perfect soulmate, questioning if settling for anything less could ever mean a lasting marriage.

Let's be more like Abram when faced with nonmoral decisions. Let's not fret about taking the best option every time or worry that our lives are doomed to failure if we go left when we could have gone right. Let's trust that **when we make pleasing God our ultimate life goal, He will care for us with eternal blessings.** (Because He can, and He will.)

QUESTIONS FOR CLARITY

Abram's journey is an example of faith and trust, fear and mistrust. As we make decisions, here are a few questions we can ask ourselves:

- How can I step out in faith even when I don't have any certainty about which way to go? Which of God's commandments can I follow when I don't receive specific directions? What promises of God can I cling to as I make my way? Do I have holy indifference, or do I insist on my own life plans?
- Have I made a wrong turn in life? Has fear led me to a poor decision? How can I remind myself that God provides me with grace and forgiveness? Where in my life have I seen how God works out everything for my good—even my missteps?
- Do I have anxiety about making the optimal choice? Do I sometimes put off making a decision because I'm afraid of making the wrong one? Can Abram's experience with Lot remind me that trusting in God's blessing and promise is more important than always making sure I'm making the best decision? Can I take comfort in knowing that God can wonderfully work even my suboptimal choices for my eternal good as I love and trust Him?

DIVINE DIRECTIONS: THE PURPOSE OF OUR JOURNEYS

When John and I set out for Missoula, we didn't know what to expect. But we stepped out in faith. Along the way, we sometimes felt tempted to turn around and go back to what was familiar and safe. Even after we had settled into our new home, loneliness occasionally made us question God's guidance.

But we ended up loving life in Missoula. I rejoiced in the million-dollar mountain view through our patio door. God blessed John's ministry at the church. And eventually, I found my footing on a path that included new friends and career opportunities.

Proverbs 3:5–6 says,

> Trust in the Lord with all your heart,
> and do not lean on your own understanding.
> In all your ways acknowledge Him,
> and He will make straight your paths.

The word *acknowledge* in this passage comes from the Hebrew word *yada,* which means "to be familiar with," "to learn to know," "to be acquainted with," and even "to know intimately." Whatever road God has placed us on, let's make the journey all about getting to know Him better. The more we know about God's character, the more peace we will have as we travel. The more we know what pleases the Lord, the more wisdom we'll have when we come to any fork in the road.

Friends, let's remember that God's purpose for all of our journeys is to increase our trust in Him. If we knew every twist and turn of our road ahead of time, would we reach for His hand to guide us or would we depend on our own navigational skills? More than knowing our specific destination, God wants us to grow in faith, trusting that He will get us there according to His plan.

Abram's life shows us that God will not abandon us on the side of the road when we stumble and fall or even deliberately take a wrong turn. He can turn our missteps into something good.

In a world where experts try to optimize our lives in everything from financial success to the right mascara, God wants to maximize our faith. Faced with seemingly unlimited choices, the stress of making the *right* decision can send us into a tailspin, but we can see how God blessed Abram even when he allowed Lot to choose the best land. Instead of focusing on making the optimal choice, let's concentrate on God's promise to travel with us, providing what we need along the way.

Let's make faith in a fantastic God the focus of our journey.

* * * * *

Eternal God,
I hear the call to follow You,
but sometimes the path seems unclear.
Can You give me
a detailed map of my life?
big yellow signs that tell me where to turn?
Perhaps You don't offer those travel guides because
instead of a detailed itinerary, You offer step-by-step directions
instead of an atlas, You provide Your presence.
Eternal God,
hold my hand as I walk this uncertain path.
In Jesus' name. Amen.

CHAPTER 2

HAGAR

Escape into the Wilderness

TIMELINE

Abram (Abraham)	ca. 2100 BC
Hagar	ca. 2081 BC

Home, here we come! We had just spent a splendid few days in the Detroit area with my husband's sister and her family. Our kids, ages 6 and 3, loved spending time at their aunt and uncle's home, which was situated on a lake. The five cousins had oodles of fun splashing in the lake during the day and roasting hot dogs and marshmallows on the beach at night. We had all enjoyed our time together, but now we needed to get home (now in Aurora, Illinois). The next day was Sunday, and we hoped to get home with enough time to unpack the car, give the kids their Saturday night baths, and crawl into bed early.

But just an hour down the road, the motor of our black station wagon suddenly stopped humming its mechanical tune and began to slow down. My husband eased the car to the side of I-94 near an overpass. He got out and looked under the hood to see if he could figure out why the car had suddenly malfunctioned. He thought the water pump had failed, a problem he could not remedy.

We were thankful that the car had quit working close to a town and not in the middle of nowhere. This was in the age before cell phones, so we needed to go in person to ask for a tow truck to take our car to a repair shop. John stayed with the car while the kids and I scrambled up the hill to the road and walked a block or two to a gas station.

We walked back to the car where we all waited. It wasn't long before a tow truck arrived and pulled our car to a repair shop. By then, we knew we weren't going to get home for the early turn-in we had planned. We simply hoped the mechanics could fix the car in time for us to drive the remaining five hours to our home before Sunday services began.

Amazingly, the shop had the water pump and timing belt our car needed, and the kind mechanics stayed late to fix the car. They saw our situation, heard the concern in our voices, and went above and beyond to help us. One of the men at the shop even drove us to a nearby restaurant so we could eat dinner while the car was being repaired.

After dinner, we spent long hours sitting on a bench in the shop, but eventually, the mechanics completed the repair, and we got back on the road at about 10:00 p.m. John and I took turns driving and sleeping. We arrived home in time to rest a little before we had to get ready for church.

Our journey had abruptly stopped at the side of the road when the car's timing belt and water pump gave out. We needed someone to repair the car.

Hagar, a servant of Sarai, also experienced some bad timing and a lack of water during her journey, but she didn't have the luxury of a tow truck and mechanics to help her. Her situation presented more than an inconvenience. She faced life-threatening problems.

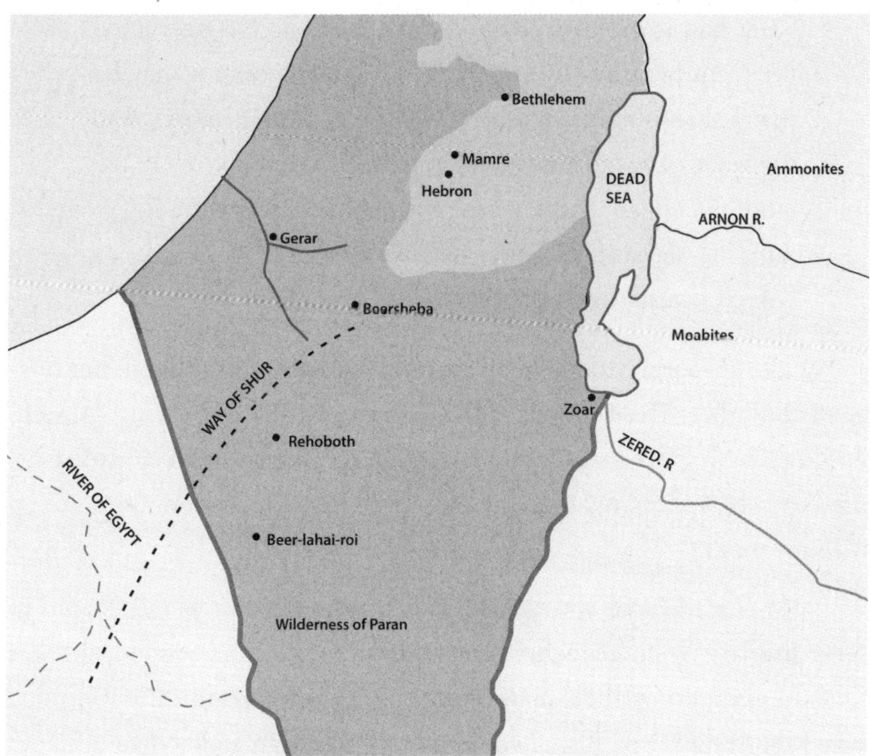

MAP © ISTOCK.COM / PETER HERMESFURIAN

SETTING THE SCENE

In chapter 1, we learned about how the patriarch Abram and his wife, Sarai, journeyed to Egypt when Canaan experienced a famine. While there, Pharaoh gave Abram "sheep, oxen, male donkeys, male servants, female servants, female donkeys, and camels" (Genesis 12:16). Hagar was most likely one of those female servants. When Pharaoh learned the truth that Sarai was Abram's wife (and not his sister), he sent Abram "away with his wife and all that he had" (v. 20). Hagar went with them whether she wanted to or not.

As we skip ahead to Genesis 16, we find that Hagar was a major character in Abram and Sarai's life:

> Now Sarai, Abram's wife, had borne him no children. She had a female Egyptian servant whose name was Hagar. And

> Sarai said to Abram, "Behold now, the LORD has prevented me from bearing children. Go in to my servant; it may be that I shall obtain children by her." And Abram listened to the voice of Sarai. So, after Abram had lived ten years in the land of Canaan, Sarai, Abram's wife, took Hagar the Egyptian, her servant, and gave her to Abram her husband as a wife. (Genesis 16:1–3)

At age 75, Sarai had given up on birthing babies, so she told her husband about her "Do it myself" plan. "It was like she was saying, 'Abram, it looks like we have to go with Plan B. If God isn't going to give me children, it seems a surrogate is my only path to motherhood. So go sleep with my maid.'"[3]

Poor Hagar! First, she was wrenched from her homeland, forced to serve this elderly couple who did not share her culture. Second, she was forced to be part of their plan to conceive a baby. (And I'll bet no one asked the servant girl if she would like to marry an eighty-five-year-old man and bear his child.) Although she may not have had any input on the plan, Hagar recognized the advantages of it when the idea worked.

> And he went in to Hagar, and she conceived. And when she saw that she had conceived, she looked with contempt on her mistress. (v. 4)

Surrogacy was a familiar practice in that time, so perhaps Hagar no longer thought of herself as just a servant because she carried her master's child. She had done something her mistress could not: conceive a baby. Perhaps after years of servitude, she couldn't pass up the chance to flaunt her new role. Before, Hagar may have been treated as unimportant and insignificant, so now she returned the favor and treated Sarai with disdain.

Sarai could not stand this behavior. Not only did she bear the pain of infertility, but she also had to watch her servant take the role she desperately wanted. And then her servant treated her like dirt.

Although Sarai had initiated the plan, she wanted to scrap it like yesterday's lunch. She took the problem to Abram, who evidently recognized a no-win situation for himself, and let Sarai do what she wanted with Hagar. So Sarai "dealt harshly with her" (v. 6). We don't know exactly what that means. Did she punish Hagar? Threaten her? In any case, the harsh treatment made Hagar run away. She fled and began a new journey back to her homeland.

HAGAR AS SURROGATE MOTHER

After reading the account of Sarai and Hagar, we may want to ask, "Sarai, what were you thinking? How could you believe introducing another woman into the marriage would solve your problem?"

But using a servant as a surrogate was common practice in the ancient world. Some marriage contracts from the second millennium BC clearly stated that if a woman could not have children, she had to offer her husband a surrogate to bear a child.

In addition, the ancient world didn't fully understand the biology of conception. They believed the male put the seed in the woman, who merely acted as an incubator for a baby. So perhaps Sarai and Abram decided one incubator was as good as another.

Although Abram and Sarai's culture accepted Sarai's solution, God wanted her to wait for His timing and plan.*

**For a Christian view on modern bioethics and reproductive technology check out Richard C. Eyer,* Holy People, Holy Lives: Law and Gospel in Bioethics *(Concordia Publishing House, 2001).*

THE JOURNEY

I imagine the scene from Genesis 16 looking like this: Tears stung Hagar's eyes as she ran from the tents of her master and mistress. How could she have thought that she mattered to them? In the years she had served this elderly couple, she had felt invisible, someone to merely wash Sarai's clothes and cook her meals. She doubted Sarai's husband, Abram, even knew her name.

Now, of course, Abram *did* know her—intimately. Yet it seemed she still did not matter. She carried the master's child, but she received cruel treatment. Yes, perhaps she should not have boasted quite so loudly. She should not have advertised her pregnancy quite so often. It turned out that although her condition had changed, her status had not. Sarai's harsh comments made her painfully aware of that. So Hagar quickly rolled her few belongings into a bundle and ran. She would go home to Egypt.

Hagar started out by running on the road to Shur, but she grew tired and shuffled her feet along the dry, barren land. Weariness and thirst slowed her steps. She shielded her eyes and scanned the way ahead. She saw only more sand, more scrawny plants, more . . . nothing. Hagar paused as she saw a tiny clump of trees. Could it mean water? She walked toward the speck of greenery. As she got closer to it, her anxiety lessened a bit, for she saw a spring in the midst of the bushes.

Hagar sat at the edge of the water and splashed some of it on her face. She filled her waterskin with the cool liquid and drank it deeply, letting it slide down her parched throat. At least she would not die of thirst. But what would happen next? How could she go any further?

Then she heard someone call her name. She looked up and saw a beautiful being, an angel sent from heaven. "Hagar, the servant of Sarai," he said. How did he know her name, her status? "Where have you come from and where are you going?"

She couldn't hide the truth: "I am running away from my mistress."

"Hagar," the angelic visitor continued, "You must return to your mistress and serve her."

Hagar thought, "Anything but that." But the visitor continued, "I will bless your son. You will call him Ishmael, for God has heard your distress. He will multiply your descendants into a great multitude."

Hagar could hardly believe what she heard. To Pharaoh, she was only a bargaining chip, but *God* saw her. To Abram and Sarai, she was a means to get what they wanted, but *God* knew her name. As tears rolled down her cheeks, Hagar responded, "You are the God who sees me!"

THE WOMAN WHO NAMED GOD

When the Lord found Hagar in the wilderness, she called Him *El-Roi*—"a God of seeing" (Genesis 16:13). She learned that God saw her need and watched over her. Because of her meeting with God, the spring she discovered in the wilderness was named Beer-lahai-roi, meaning "well of the Living One seeing me." How amazing that the servant girl of Sarai was the only woman in the Bible who gave God a name!

THE GOD WHO SEES

As a slave, Hagar may have felt invisible, an insignificant servant to wash dishes or mend Sarai's clothes. When Sarai came up with her plan to have Hagar bear her and Abram a son, she probably didn't consult her servant girl. And even after she conceived, Hagar may have felt the baby mattered to Abram and Sarai. But the woman who carried the baby? She may have still felt unseen.

So when the Angel of the Lord surprised her in the wilderness and called her by name, she could hardly believe God noticed her. God saw her in her desperate situation! He also saw the future He had planned for her, and that future held hope. Not only would God bless her with a son, but He would make that child into a great nation. After feeling hidden for so long, Hagar's heart was probably filled with joy at the realization that God had seen her all along.

Sometimes the most difficult stretches of our journeys happen when we feel unseen. We all have wilderness times in our lives, times when we feel like running away. But when those difficulties are compounded with the feeling that no one cares about us or understands us, it may feel as if it is almost too much to bear.

So, dear friends, remember this: God sees you. Just as He saw Hagar in the wilderness, He sees you sitting by the hospital bed. He sees you when your car breaks down on the side of the road. He sees you agonizing over the family budget. He sees you as you sit alone at home again. **We can take comfort when our life journeys take us into the wilderness because God still sees us and looks after us.**

ANGEL OF THE LORD

Did you know that the account of Hagar contains the first mention of an angel in the Bible? The Hebrew word for angel, *mal'ak*, means "messenger." It usually indicates a created being that speaks for God. But when the text uses the term "angel of the LORD" interchangeably with "the LORD" as it does in Genesis 16:7–14, it "signals an appearance of God's Son before His incarnation."* These special manifestations of God on earth are called *theophanies*. "Theophanies remind us that God sustains His creation and that His personal, active participation in human history continued after the fall."**

How interesting that God gave the honor of seeing the preincarnate Christ to a woman whom many saw as a nobody.

* TLSB, *"Old Testament Names for God."*
** TLSB, *"Theophanies in Genesis."*

Perhaps one of the reasons Hagar left was because she couldn't stand feeling invisible for one more day. So she made an impulsive decision that put her and her unborn child at risk. Sometimes I have consciously or unconsciously made choices solely based on what would get me noticed.

But what if I remember that God sees me? That He notices me when I *serve* on a committee and not just when I chair it? That He sees me when I cook dinner for my family and not just when I speak to a room full of people? Perhaps the truth of His loving gaze will help me choose the tasks and positions that suit the gifts He gave me, even if that leaves me in the wings instead of on center stage. Maybe the joy of His constant attention will enable me to say no to opportunities that will harm my most important relationships, even if those opportunities advance my career, status, or bank account.

Sisters, let's take comfort in the fact that God sees us. He invites us to drink from the well of living water welling up from His Son, Jesus.

WHEN GOD SAYS, "STAY"

When the Angel of the Lord asked Hagar where she had come from and where she was going, Hagar honestly admitted she was running away from her mistress. She knew where she had come from, but she had no idea where she was going. God's Messenger informed her of her destination: "Return to your mistress" (Genesis 16:9). Hagar would make a round-trip journey from an unbearable situation and back again.

Sometimes God tells us to stay in a place we would like to get away from. I distinctly remember a dream I had when I felt overwhelmed with parenting and homeschooling my young kids. I dreamed that another homeschool mom and I decided we would book a three-week cruise. (Bermuda, here we come!) We wanted to flee our humdrum lives for something more exciting, more exotic. My friend and I laughed over that dream, but sometimes waking up to another day of doing laundry and teaching fractions seemed a cruel reality. Nevertheless, God asked me to stay in that role of homeschool mom for fifteen years, and it turned out to be a great blessing.

Of course, there are times when leaving is the best choice. If you are living with an unfaithful or abusive spouse, it is time to go, not time to stay. Be assured that you can speak privately with your pastor, a Christian counselor, or trained employees and volunteers at a women's shelter to find help. And be comforted that forgiveness is secured by the cross of Christ.

But consider that God places us in our current city with our particular people for a reason that may be unclear to us in the present. I have heard this advice from several wise people: If God doesn't give a clear indication to leave, the place He wants you to be is where you are right now.

WHERE HAVE YOU COME FROM AND WHERE ARE YOU GOING?

When the Angel of the Lord appeared to Hagar on the road to Shur, the first thing he said was, "Hagar, servant of Sarai, where have you come from and where are you going?" (v. 8).

On our drive from Detroit to Chicago that evening, we knew where we had come from and where we were going, but along the way, our car's timing belt broke, and we found ourselves stranded. In our life journeys, we may also feel stuck and wonder if the timing of our lives is severely broken. When that happens, perhaps we can use the questions the angel asked Hagar to determine our next steps.

First, we can ask ourselves, "Where have I come from? Where have I seen God work in my life in the past? When have I seen God use the talents and abilities He gave me? How have my past struggles and successes shaped me to help others?" When we see where we have come from, perhaps the way ahead becomes a little clearer. **We may discern where we are going by remembering where we have been.**

Next, we can ask, "Where am I going?" Right after the Angel of the Lord asked Hagar this question, he gave her a destination: "Return to your mistress and submit to her" (v. 9). He gave short-term instructions to return and submit. The word *submit* is from the Hebrew word *ana*, meaning "to humble oneself," "to become low." God asks us to submit to His will, to humble ourselves; this may mean that we accept a situation that chafes against our pride.

However, right after those short-term instructions, the Angel of the Lord gave Hagar a long-term promise: "I will surely multiply your offspring so that they cannot be numbered for multitude" (v. 10). Although Hagar felt all alone in the moment, God would bless her with descendants beyond numbering. When we feel stuck in an isolating situation, we can cling to God's promises for a glorious future.

REMEMBER TO PACK: A REFLECTION PRACTICE

When making decisions for the future, reflecting on the past can give us perspective and direction. At the end of every month, I take time to look back and list the highs and lows, the successes and struggles of the past thirty days or so. Not only does this help me see that I actually accomplished something that month, but it enables me to notice what brought me joy and what created frustration. When I take time to notice how the community service organization that used to bring joy now causes exasperation, it helps me make the decision to let that activity go.

I encourage you to take time for reflection. Ask yourself these questions: What filled me with joy? What habits were helpful? What energized me? What depleted me? What did I find frustrating? What you discover may help you discern what to say yes to and what to say no to in the future.

Hear God's voice ask, "Where have you come from?" As you reflect on that question, ask the Holy Spirit to provide you with peace and insight about where you are going.

Paul tells us in 2 Corinthians 4:17, "For this light momentary affliction is preparing for us an eternal weight of glory beyond all comparison." And in Romans 8:18, "For I consider that the sufferings of this present time are not worth comparing with the glory that is to be revealed to us."

I'm not trying to minimize the trauma Hagar went through or the painful experiences we encounter in this broken world, but considering what God has waiting for us can help us in the meantime. And when God asks us to return and submit, humbly accepting life as it is, we can be assured that God continually works behind the scenes to weave the ordinary and difficult days into something extraordinary and beautiful.

Let's remember God's long-term promises for our future: "In My Father's house are many rooms. If it were not so, would I have told you that I go to prepare a place for you?" (John 14:2). When we consider what steps to take in the short-term, let's always consider our ultimate destination. How can an eternal perspective help us as we make plans for our next weeks, months, and years?

GOD WILL OPEN YOUR EYES

After Hagar's encounter with the Angel of the Lord, she returned to her place as Sarai's servant. Genesis 16:15 tells us, "And Hagar bore Abram a son, and Abram called the name of his son, whom Hagar bore, Ishmael."

According to several commentators, approximately seventeen years had passed by the time Hagar is next mentioned in Scripture. In the meantime, God changed her master's name from Abram, meaning "exalted father," to Abraham, "father of many nations." Yahweh also changed Sarai's name to Sarah, which means "princess." The Lord reiterated His promise to greatly multiply Abraham, and although Abraham and Sarah laughed at the thought of a one-hundred-year-old man and ninety-year-old woman having a baby, God was true to His word. When Hagar's son, Ishmael, was about fourteen years old, Abraham and Sarah's boy, Isaac, whose name means "laughter," was born.

Hagar enters the scene again in Genesis 21. Abraham had planned a big party to celebrate the weaning of Isaac. If Sarah had followed Middle Eastern customs of the time, Isaac would have been about three years old (and Ishmael seventeen). Imagine all the neighbors arriving, laughing, and slapping Abraham on the back with hearty congratulations. But over in the corner of the camp, Sarah saw another kind of laughter—the teenage Ishmael mocking Isaac. Sarah could not stand this treatment of her son. She immediately went to Abraham and told him to get rid of Hagar and Ishmael.

This seems like a drastic reaction to a bit of sibling rivalry, but perhaps this incident was the last straw in a heap of insults and disrespect. God indicated that Ishmael would "be a wild donkey of a man, his hand against everyone" (Genesis 16:12), and perhaps Ishmael had already lived up to that reputation.

Sarah's new idea "was very displeasing to Abraham on account of his son" (Genesis 21:11). Sarah didn't always have the best advice, but God said, "Whatever Sarah says to you, do as she tells you, for through Isaac shall your offspring be named. And I will make a nation of the son of the slave woman also, because he is your offspring" (vv. 12–13). "Though Sarah's motives may have been mixed, God approved of her counsel" (*TLSB*, note on Genesis 21:12).

Still, the next scene seems particularly heartbreaking. Early the next morning, Abraham gave Hagar some bread and a skin of water and sent her and Ishmael away. Why didn't he at least provide them with a donkey loaded with a pack of supplies for the journey? Why not arrange for protection for their wilderness wanderings?

Again, Hagar found herself traveling. Did she walk into the wilderness, eyes blurred with tears? Did she look back toward the camp, hoping Abraham would change his mind and call them back? Did her heart beat wildly in the fear of not knowing how she and her son would survive?

Hagar wandered in the wilderness of Beersheba, but eventually the water in the skin ran out. Now they had nothing. Hagar didn't want to watch Ishmael die, so "she put the child under one of the bushes" (v. 15) while she went off "about the distance of a bowshot" (v. 16)—perhaps fifty to one hundred yards.

What a heartrending scene. Surely Hagar thought this meant the end of her journey. Hagar wept, feeling hopeless and helpless. God called out to Hagar from heaven, "What troubles you, Hagar? Fear not, for God has heard the voice of the boy where he is. Up! Lift up the boy, and hold him fast with your hand, for I will make him into a great nation" (vv. 17–18). God heard Ishmael—a real-life fulfillment of his name, which means "God hears."

Then God opened Hagar's eyes, and she saw a well of water. Had her eyes been too clouded with tears to see it before? Had despair prevented her from seeing a solution that had existed all along? We may not wander in a desert with an empty water bottle, but in the wilderness times of our lives, discouragement and hopelessness may act like blinders to how God is working. Pain may blind us to God's grace. Hurt may turn our gaze inward. But God continues to work in our lives—even in the wilderness. He continues to provide living water to quench our spiritual thirst. When we, like Hagar, cannot see a way forward in our journey, we can ask God to open our eyes to His provision and be assured that He will point us to His thirst-quenching Word. He may reveal a new possibility for a job when it seems all options have been exhausted. He may provide the name of a new doctor and point to the Great Physician when all hope of healing has been lost. He may put a new friend in your path when loneliness has been your only companion. **When you cannot see a way forward in your journey, ask God to open your eyes to His provision.**

The water revived and refreshed Hagar and Ishmael enough to allow them to continue their journey. Scripture informs us that they eventually settled in the wilderness of Paran, which lies in the Sinai Peninsula, close to Hagar's original homeland: Egypt.

Just as God provided sustenance for Hagar, He will provide divine direction for us in our wilderness seasons.

REMEMBER TO PACK: REFRESHMENT FOR YOUR SOUL

When Hagar had given up all hope of moving forward on her journey and expected death to take her and Ishmael, God opened her eyes. Suddenly she noticed a well she had not seen before.

Sometimes we don't see God's offer of refreshment either. The Lord's Supper is "a pure, wholesome, comforting remedy that grants salvation and comfort. It will cure you and give you life both in soul and body."*

Lord Jesus, help us not take for granted the gift of life-renewing forgiveness in this Sacrament. Open our eyes to the soul-refreshing grace You offer. Amen.

**Large Catechism, Part 5, paragraph 68.*

DIVINE DIRECTIONS: GOD SEES ALL OUR WAYS

In Psalm 139, King David praised God for His all-seeing power:

> O Lord, You have searched me and known me!
> You know when I sit down and when I rise up;
> You discern my thoughts from afar.
> You search out my path and my lying down
> and are acquainted with all my ways. (vv. 1–3)

Hagar experienced God tending to her needs. Twice she ended up in the desert confused and distressed. But she also experienced the presence of God twice. Twice the Lord saw her desperate situation and pointed her to a solution. He was acquainted with all her ways. Few people in the Bible saw the Angel of the Lord. Few experienced two theophanies.

Few received specific instructions from God about the next steps of their journeys.

When you feel abandoned and alone, remember that Jesus always sees you. He is acquainted with all your ways. He sees your pain, your struggle. Although it may feel like no one else notices you, His gaze constantly follows you.

God also discerns your thoughts from afar. He can help you sort out the jumbled anxieties and uncertainties rolling around in your mind. Perhaps He asks you the same question He asked Hagar: "Where have you come from and where are you going?" Remembering how God has guided and supported you in the past can give you hope and direction for the future. And fixing your eyes on the ultimate destination of heaven can relieve any apprehensions about the current uphill road you travel on. What's more, God has provided you with the constancy of His Word, where you can be reminded that He fulfills His promises for you and will bring to fruition the good plan He has for you.

The Lord has already planned out the path ahead of you. When you find yourself unable to see the way forward, pray that God will open your eyes to His miraculous provision and trust that He is with you through the difficult times in this earthly life. Rejoice in the fact that He promises to refresh you continuously with His living water: Jesus.

Revel in the God who sees you on every step of your journey.

QUESTIONS FOR CLARITY

Hagar's journey offers us hope when our own journeys feel like wilderness treks and we wonder if we are alone in our struggles. As we make decisions for our lives, here are a few questions we can ask ourselves:

- **How does remembering that God sees me on my journey help me navigate the twists and turns of life?** As I recall that Christ always notices me, can I avoid making choices based solely on what will bring me attention? How can a wilderness time help me see Christ more clearly?
- **Where have I come from and where am I going?** Where have I seen God work in my life in the past? How can this inform current decisions? How can remembering my ultimate destination of heaven help me make wise choices now?
- **When I feel stuck, do pain and heartache blind me to what God has already provided?** How can I remember to pray for God to open my eyes to His life-giving provision?

* * * * *

O God of seeing,
I often feel
unseen,
invisible.
Yet Your Word assures me that Your loving
gaze finds me when I'm
lost,
confused,
alone.
The knowledge of Your ever-seeing vision and
caring attention fill me with
wonder,
hope,

strength.
O God of seeing,
my heart has long echoed the questions
where have I come from?
where am I going?
I yearn for
a detailed map for my steps,
specific directions for a meaningful life.
But then I realize that even more wonderful
than knowing
exactly where I'm going in the next year,
the next decade,
is the knowledge that
You are with me in the journey.
You see everything that lies ahead.
You hold my hand and lead the way.
O God of seeing,
thank You for seeing me.
In Jesus' name. Amen.

CHAPTER 3

REBEKAH

A Path to a New Life

TIMELINE

Abram (Abraham)	ca. 2100 BC
Hagar	ca. 2081 BC
Rebekah	ca. 2026 BC

My father pulled the car to a stop, took one look at our surroundings, and asked me, "Are you sure you want to do this?"

We had driven almost two hundred miles from our relatively small hometown of Wausau, Wisconsin, to the big city of Milwaukee. The car was stuffed with my suitcases because I was about to embark on a yearlong adventure traveling the country with the Christian musical group Joy Inc.

When I found out I had made the group, I could barely contain my excitement. I would have the privilege of doing what I loved—singing and playing the piano—while getting to see the whole country. My father did not share my enthusiasm. His parental concern for my safety overrode any thrill he may have had for me about this new opportunity. Those

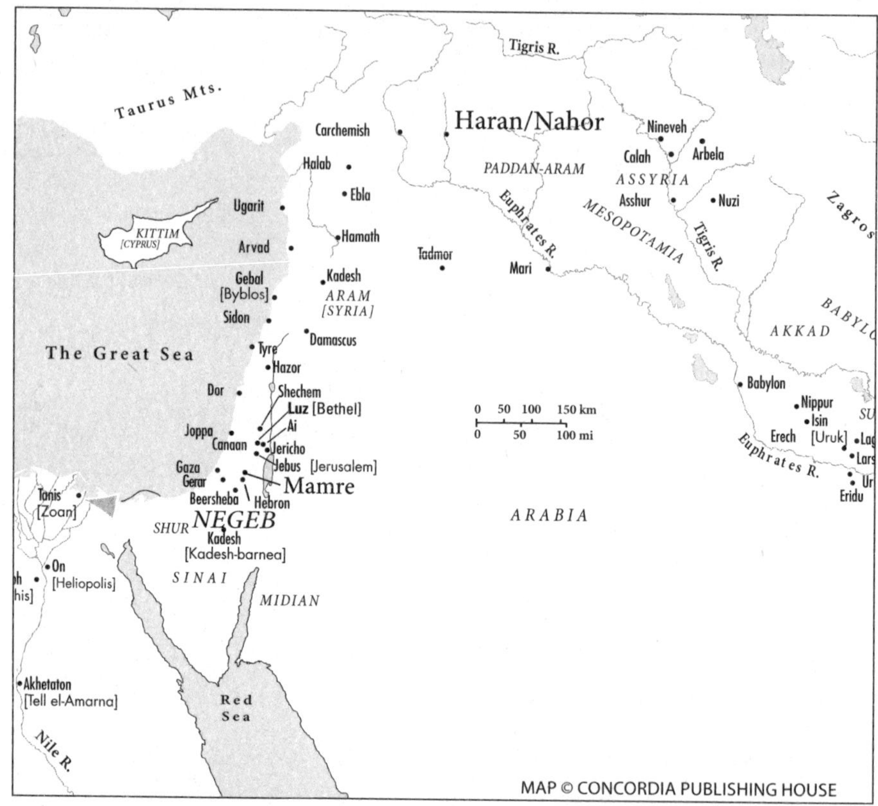

concerns multiplied when he stopped the car at the address the director of the group had given us for the Joy House, the home base of the musical group. The seventeen members of the group would live here during a month of rehearsals. While the house was an old but well-preserved Victorian home, the rest of the neighborhood looked run-down, dilapidated, and even a little scary. My dad had serious misgivings about leaving me in such a place.

But I was determined. When I received the invitation to travel with Joy Inc., I had said, "I will go," and I wouldn't back out now. So my father helped me haul my suitcases up the wooden steps to the gingerbread-embellished front porch and we rang the doorbell. The director opened the door to me, my dad, and the rest of my family, who had come along to see me off. We stepped into the house and engaged in small talk for a while, but eventually the time came for my family to leave and drive the two hundred miles back home.

Suddenly, they had gone, and I found myself on a path to a new life.

SETTING THE SCENE

Rebekah also bravely took a path to a new life. Her story in Scripture began about thirty-seven years after Hagar wandered in the wilderness of Beersheba.

When Hagar left Abraham and Sarah, Isaac was probably about age 3. About thirty-four years later, Sarah died at the age of 127. Perhaps her death made Abraham realize that he must get his affairs in order. Most important, he needed to find a wife for Isaac, who was close to 40. The patriarch did not want Isaac, the son of promise, to intermarry with the surrounding Canaanites, so he sent his oldest, most faithful servant on a mission to find Isaac a wife.

Abraham told his servant,

> Put your hand under my thigh, that I may make you swear by the Lord, the God of heaven and God of the earth, that you will not take a wife for my son from the daughters of the Canaanites, among whom I dwell. (Genesis 24:2–3)

We might think, "Uh. Put my hand under your thigh? Couldn't a handshake suffice?" But it seems this form of making an oath was standard practice, especially for such serious business. Abraham would release the servant from his oath if the potential spouse refused to come back with him. But under no circumstance would the servant find Isaac a wife who was from Canaan.

So the servant loaded up ten of Abraham's camels with "all sorts of choice gifts from his master" (v. 10). These gifts would pay the bride price and demonstrate Isaac's ability to support a wife. (Plus, if the girl he found had a closet like mine, he would need one camel just to transport her shoes.) Once everything was in order, he journeyed to Mesopotamia, to the city of Nahor (see v. 10). Some commentators think that the servant went all the way back to Ur, but most think Nahor was in the vicinity of Haran, where Abraham and his father, Terah, lived for a while.

We have already learned from Abraham's journey that the distance between Canaan and Haran was approximately five hundred miles, a distance that would have taken about a month to travel one way. Abraham traveled south to Canaan, and his servant traveled in the opposite direction.

THE JOURNEY

Here's how I imagine the scene: Rebekah swayed with the rhythm of her camel's steps and wondered if this journey would ever end. Almost a month had passed since she left home. A month of sitting atop a smelly camel. Talk about saddle sore!

Rebekah recalled the day she first met the servant who now led the caravan heading south. The day had started out like any other. But when she went to the well that evening, she noticed a stranger—with ten camels. He had politely asked her for a sip of water, which she immediately gave him. Her mother's instructions about hospitality echoed in her mind, so she offered to draw water for the camels too. What had she been thinking? She had forgotten how much a camel could drink. It most likely took nearly one hundred trips down the steps to the well and back before those thirsty dromedaries were satisfied.

Rebekah had thought that was the end of her interaction with the stranger, but it was only the beginning. The man responded to her work by giving her a gold ring and two gold bracelets. Those pieces could easily represent a year's wages. The man then asked about her family and if they might have room for him to spend the night. Rebekah explained that she was the daughter of Bethuel, a relative of Abraham, and that they had plenty of room for him, plus straw for the animals.

Then the man did a surprising thing. He bowed his head and worshiped God.

Rebekah ran to tell her mother all that happened. When her brother, Laban, saw the riches on her arm, he ran to the well and brought the generous stranger home. They welcomed him with something to eat.

Although the servant's stomach surely complained with hunger, he said he wanted to tell them the purpose of his trip before he took a bite.

The whole family leaned forward to listen as the visitor said, "I am the servant of Abraham. The Lord has blessed my master with many flocks, herds, and servants. He has only one son, and he sent me here to you, his family, to find a wife for that son. Abraham does not want Isaac to marry a Canaanite woman.

"I asked the Lord to give me a sign of the right woman for my master's son. 'Please, Lord,' I prayed. 'When I am standing by a spring and ask a young woman for a drink, may she also offer to draw water for the camels.'

"Then Rebekah came with her water jar and did just as I had prayed. When I found out that you, her father, are Abraham's nephew, I knew God had answered my prayer.

"So now, what do you think? Are you willing to give Rebekah in marriage to my master's son, or should I look elsewhere?"

While her father and brother agreed that God's hand seemed to orchestrate the marriage, Rebekah could hardly take it all in. Before she could offer her opinion on the matter, the men said, "Take her and go" (v. 51). What had begun as a simple offer of a sip of water had now become a betrothal. A betrothal to a man she had never met!

She left with Abraham's servant the next day. During those many days on the road, her emotions swayed back and forth almost as often as the camel's gait. One moment, excitement exploded in her heart as she thought about her new circumstances. The next instant, doubt filled her mind as she wondered what her new life would look like.

Just then she looked toward the horizon and saw a man walking toward them. When the servant told her that the approaching man was her future husband, she slid off the camel. (Oh dear. After so many days on that animal, could she still walk?) She then covered herself with her veil and walked toward Isaac and a new life.

ANCIENT WELLS

When you read about Rebekah at the well of Nahor, you might picture her at a round stone well, cranking a bucket up and down to fill it with water. But ancient wells were far below ground—as much as 190 feet—and accessed by stone steps. Rebekah would have had to descend and ascend these stairs many times. Her jar may have weighed 15 pounds or more and held as much as 3 gallons that weighed up to 25 pounds. A camel can drink as much as 25 gallons. Do the math: 10 camels = 250 gallons. She would have made almost a hundred trips up and down the steps to quench the thirst of Abraham's animals.*

* *See Liz Curtis Higgs,* Slightly Bad Girls of the Bible: Flawed Women Loved by a Flawless God *(Waterbrook Press, 2007), 95–96.*

DEPEND ON GOD

Rebekah's journey began with Abraham's servant's journey. Abraham gave his most trusted helper the significant task of finding a wife for his son. God had called Abraham and his future descendants to Canaan, and the patriarch didn't want his son to leave—even temporarily. Abraham's faith in Yahweh must have had some effect on the servant, for the servant did not try to accomplish the important matchmaking by his own efforts. When he arrived at Nahor in the evening—the time women came to draw water—he parked his camels at the well. He prayed to Yahweh:

> O LORD, God of my master Abraham, please grant me success today and show steadfast love to my master Abraham. Behold, I am standing by the spring of water, and the daughters of the men of the city are coming out to draw water. Let the young woman to whom I shall say, "Please let down your jar that I may drink," and who shall say, "Drink, and I will water your camels"—let her be the one whom You have appointed for Your servant Isaac. By this I shall know that You have shown steadfast love to my master. (vv. 12–14)

God graciously answered his prayer. Before he even finished praying, Rebekah came out, and she drew water for all ten of his thirsty animals. Here was a hardworking and generous woman. Further questions informed the servant that she came from Abraham's clan. The servant immediately responded in worship:

> The man bowed his head and worshiped the LORD and said, "Blessed be the LORD, the God of my master Abraham, who has not forsaken His steadfast love and His faithfulness toward my master. As for me, the LORD has led me in the way to the house of my master's kinsmen." (vv. 26–27)

We can learn a lot from this servant. His prayers offer a wealth of insight we can use in our life journeys.

Begin your journey with prayer. Abraham's servant started his search in Nahor by praying that God would give him success. He displayed a dependence on God, not on his own wisdom. When I have a choice to make, I often forget this essential step—until I fall flat on my face. *Lord, help me turn to You first, asking You for success in my journey and the wisdom to make the right choice. In Jesus' name. Amen.*

Rely on God's steadfast love and faithfulness. In both of his prayers, Abraham's servant recited these two qualities of Yahweh. When faced with decisions that stir up anxiety in my soul, nothing calms that angst quite like remembering God's unfailing love toward me. If He loves me enough to sacrifice His Son, certainly I can count on that love to guide me. Psalm 25:10 says, "All the paths of the LORD are steadfast love and faithfulness, for those who keep His covenant and His testimonies." God promises that *all* the roads He has laid out for me are mapped by His care. *Thank You, Lord, for reminding me that I can count on You to provide Your grace and love as I cling to Your promises, even though the path ahead might have a few potholes and some steep hills. In Jesus' name. Amen.*

SHOULD I PRAY FOR A SIGN?

Abraham's servant prayed for a specific sign: "May the woman I ask for a drink of water and who volunteers to water my camels be the woman You have chosen for Isaac." God answered the servant's prayer even before he had said "Amen."

Does this mean we should pray for a sign when we search for the right choice? To find the answer, let's look at the servant's prayer. His strategy was similar to the ancient practice of seeking oracles when a person would ask a deity a yes-or-no question and the god would answer through things such as the casting of lots, inspecting the entrails of a sacrificial animal, or (as in this case) arranging for an unusual occurrence.*

However, this practice happened only a few times in the Bible (see Joshua 18; 1 Samuel 14) and was used in an era when people did not have God's written Word to guide them. Later in the history of God's people, God told His will through the priests' use of the Urim and Thummin—devices priests used to understand God's will for Israel. After that, God spoke through His prophets.

It may seem tempting to ask God for specific guidance in this way. ("Lord, bless this coin toss. If it lands tails side up, I'll know You want me to move to Seattle. If it's heads, I'll go to Birmingham.") This appears to give an immediate answer when we feel we're drowning in a sea of uncertainty. But this approach attempts to force God to act in a certain way: "Lord, I want You to do this or that." Instead, let's wait for the sovereign God to work things out in His own wise and miraculous way. Let's use His written Word to guide our route. Let's rely on the Holy Spirit, who guides all baptized children of God from within.

* *See* NIV Cultural Backgrounds Study Bible: Bringing to Life the Ancient World of Scripture *(Zondervan, 2017), note on Genesis 24:14.*

Respond in worship. As soon as the servant realized God had answered his prayer, he bowed his head in thanksgiving. For years, my family began all our car trips with a prayer for safe travel, but we often forgot to say, "Thanks, Lord," when we returned home and pulled into our driveway. *Lord, help me remember to give You thanks and praise as often as I make requests. Help me follow the example of Abraham's servant and faithfully worship You along the way as You guide me step by step. In Jesus' name. Amen.*

DO NOT BE CONFORMED TO THE WORLD

When I decided to travel the country with a Christian musical group, my life took an unusual path. All my friends headed off to college, majoring in engineering, premed, and even German. My father worried that if I didn't go to college right after high school, I might get sidetracked and never go. My high school teachers and counselors probably questioned my choice. I acted counterculturally.

When Abraham wanted to find a wife for Isaac, he also acted counterculturally. Practically speaking, it would have made more sense for Isaac to marry a Canaanite girl from a nearby influential family, forming an alliance with his neighbors and perhaps attaining a bit of the Canaanite land. But Abraham most likely knew that his family needed to be distinct from the people around him. Intermarriage with the surrounding pagan people could easily tempt Abraham and his family to assimilate rather than remain set apart. So he sent his servant to find a wife from among his relatives.

In our own life journeys, we constantly face the choice to fit in with our modern culture or to behave differently. Will we give in to the pressure to have our children play sports on Sundays, or will we make worshiping together as a family on Sundays a priority? Will we accept the world's standards in our choices of entertainment, or will we be more selective, following God's values?

Our culture will constantly attempt to shape our attitudes in both overt and subtle ways. We may not even notice how advertising and media work to bend our thinking. In Romans, the apostle Paul tells us,

> Do not be conformed to this world, but be transformed by the renewal of your mind, that by testing you may discern what is the will of God, what is good and acceptable and perfect. (Romans 12:2)

In other words, don't let the world mold you into its shape.

Like Abraham, we need to take steps to avoid assimilation into our culture. One of my mentors told me once that whenever she faced a problem or a difficult decision, she always prayed, "Lord, how do You want me to think about this?" Even though the world tries to sculpt our beliefs, the all-powerful Spirit living within can help us resist the squeeze of culture and reshape our minds. He can help us discern "what is good and acceptable and perfect." Taking a closer look at the words *good*, *acceptable*, and *perfect* can help us as we try to make difficult decisions.

> The word *good* comes from the Greek word *agathos*, meaning "pleasant," "agreeable," "joyful," "happy," "useful," and "honorable." When we have a choice to make, we can filter our options with these words. Of course, we always try to choose what is happy and pleasant. But we can also ask, "Which choice is more useful? What is more honorable?"

> We derive the word *acceptable* in Romans 12:2 from the Greek *euarestos*, meaning "well-pleasing." When we're at a fork in the road, we can ask, "Which path would please God more?"
>
> The word *perfect* comes from the important Greek term *telios*. The Greek word doesn't necessarily mean perfect in the sense of "without flaws," but it does denote something as "finished," "complete," and "mature." The Holy Spirit may choose roads with more than a few speed bumps, but He will always lead us toward greater maturity in Christ.

In our life journeys, we may be tempted to take the path that everyone else chooses. But like Abraham, let's not try to fit in with the culture around us. **Let's ask the Lord to renew our minds from within and resist the influence of the world.** Let's ignore the values of current society and ask, "Lord, how do *You* want me to think about this?"

I WILL GO

When I left home to travel with Joy Inc., the experience was both exciting and a little scary. Homesickness parked in my heart the moment I saw my family drive off. But soon I had the thrill of meeting the rest of the band members and the joy of learning new music. After a month of rehearsing our concert numbers, we had a repertoire of songs ready to perform, and we headed out on the road. Every morning, we would get up, pack our suitcases, and load them on good old Miracle White (a retrofitted school bus painted white that served as our tour bus). Someone would ask, "Where to today?" and the bus would travel to Bradley, Illinois; Louisville, Kentucky; Salt Lake City, Utah. When we arrived at the church where we would perform that evening, we would set up our instruments and sound system. At 7:00 p.m., we would sing and play our hearts out. Then we would visit with concertgoers afterward. Host families from the church generously gave us places to rest our weary heads for the night. And the next day, we'd start the process all over again.

We each had to agree, "I will go," every day.

REMEMBER TO PACK: YOUR INTUITIVE MIND

Abraham's servant wanted a quick decision: Would Rebekah leave tomorrow? When I find myself in a situation that needs a fast judgment, I often panic. I feel I don't have enough time to weigh all my options in order to make the best choice.

But God has beautifully created our minds in two parts—the rational brain and the intuitive brain. Scientific research shows that using our intuitive brain can help speed up our decision-making process. Studies indicate that participants who have less time to make a complex decision have less regret than those given more time. This happens because our prefrontal cortex, responsible for rational thought, excels at making calculations and evaluations, but only up to a point. When faced with too many variables, it gets overwhelmed. But the intuitive part of the brain can process information much quicker (eleven million bits per second versus fifty bits per second for the rational part). Therefore, making a decision using "intuition" can be more accurate than a conscious choice.

To put this into practice, scientists suggest using your rational brain to collect the information you need to make a decision but not trying to analyze it. Instead, take a break and let your intuitive mind process the data. Often this will lead to the best decision.* It's why "sleeping on it" often works!

**See "How To Make A Difficult Decision: Surprising Research Can Help," Wise Insights (website), accessed June 14, 2024, https://www.wiseinsights.net/how-to-make-a-difficult-decision.*

When Rebekah met Abraham's servant at the well, she never expected to leave home the very next day. Was she shocked when her father and brother consented to the marriage so quickly? The men in her family said, "The thing has come from the Lord; we cannot speak to you bad or good. Behold, Rebekah is before you; take her and go, and let her be the wife of your master's son, as the LORD has spoken" (Genesis 24:50–51).

The next morning, Abraham's servant announced, "Send me away to my master" (v. 54). Rebekah's family tried to stall him, saying, "Let the young woman remain with us a while, at least ten days; after that she may go" (v. 55). I can certainly understand this request. If my daughter was moving to a new home and I might never see her again, I'd like to squeeze out a little more time for hugs and goodbyes. And I think I'd like to know this servant guy a bit better before I handed my precious child over to him. Could I actually trust his story?

But the servant continued to press them: "Do not delay me, since the LORD has prospered my way. Send me away that I may go to my master" (v. 56). Finally, the family consulted Rebekah, and she said, "I will go" (v. 58). Rebekah bravely said yes. The Lord had given her a divine direction, and she agreed to step into His plan.

Rebekah said, "I will go," even though the five-hundred-mile journey would have hardship. Even though it meant leaving her family. Even though it meant leaving her familiar way of life behind.

May we, like Rebekah, say, "I will go," when Jesus asks us to follow Him. May we tell Him every day, "Yes, Lord, I will follow You even if it's inconvenient or uncomfortable. I will follow You even when it means surrendering things dear to me. I will continually step forward with You, even when I'd like to go back to what is familiar and safe."

Following Jesus is not a three-week vacation. It's a lifelong expedition of saying, "Yes, Jesus. I will go."

DIVINE DIRECTIONS: GOD LEADS IN LOVE

When Rebekah reached the end of her journey, she experienced what may have been the quickest wedding ever! The Bible tells us that right after she slid off her camel and met Isaac, he married her by taking her into his deceased mother's tent. No chance to don special wedding clothes. No opportunity to plan a sumptuous meal. No time to invite the neighbors. Not even an hour to freshen up after spending a month on a camel!

Young girls often dream of a lavish wedding. Did Rebekah plan on having a special day? If so, she never got it. But she did receive something more important: Isaac's love. Genesis 24:67 says, "Then Isaac brought her into the tent of Sarah his mother and took Rebekah, and she became his wife, and he loved her." Even though their marriage was arranged, Isaac loved Rebekah. This passage is one of the few times the Bible mentions a specific husband loving his wife. Isaac's love for Rebekah was noteworthy.

Like Rebekah, we may have to endure an arduous journey to meet our Bridegroom, Jesus. But He assures us of His love in His Word. And thankfully, we can enjoy this love during our trek through life. Throughout our lives, may we follow the example of Abraham's servant, asking God to guide our decisions. May we respond with praise and thanksgiving when we witness His guiding hand.

As we travel through life, let's ignore the world's continual manipulation of our thinking. May we not allow our culture to influence the path we take. May we not be afraid to take the road God directs us to take, even if everyone else chooses another path. May we wholeheartedly tell God, "I will go," even though following Christ may involve sacrifice. Let's reaffirm our willingness to obey and walk in Jesus' steps every day, because we know He leads in love.

QUESTIONS FOR CLARITY

Rebekah's journey and the example of Abraham's servant give us wisdom in discerning God's path for our lives. Consider these questions when making life decisions—big and small.

- **Has my journey so far exhibited a dependence on God?** Or do I tend to travel in my own strength? How can I incorporate the spiritual habits of prayer and worship in my day? How does relying on God's steadfast love and faithfulness influence my journey?
- **In what areas of life do I tend to allow my culture to influence my decisions?** Do I sometimes feel uncomfortable to stand out as a follower of Christ? How can discerning what is good help me decide?
- **Do I share Rebekah's willingness to say, "I will go,"** even if it means sacrifice? Leaving something beloved behind? Changing my priorities? How can the assurance of the Bridegroom's love help me say, "I will go"?

* * * * *

Holy Spirit,
in the depths of my heart, I want to say, "I will go."
But sometimes
I let the pull of the world distract me.
I fear the road You choose will be rocky
and hard.
I want to stay in what feels familiar
and safe.
Give me strength to step out in faith
with You because
Your faithfulness will always go with me.
Your steadfast love is my constant companion.
Every day, help me respond to Your invitation with the words
"Yes, Lord. I will go."
In Jesus' name. Amen.

CHAPTER 4

MOSES AND THE PEOPLE OF ISRAEL

Exodus from Slavery

TIMELINE

Abram (Abraham)	ca. 2100 BC
Hagar	ca. 2081 BC
Rebekah	ca. 2026 BC
Moses and the exodus	1446 BC

Our suitcases and backpacks seemed to get heavier and heavier as my husband and I wound our way through the airport in Frankfurt, Germany. Our flight from Chicago had arrived at one terminal, but our connecting flight to Beijing, China, would be leaving from another. As we followed the signs through a maze of other terminals, dark corridors, and seemingly endless hallways, we wondered if we would ever arrive at our gate. Our jet-lagged, bone-weary bodies complained as we trudged through at least two miles of passageways. But we had no choice. We needed to make that flight.

You see, we were traveling to China to visit our daughter and her family. During the ten years that they lived there, my husband and I made six journeys to see them. Usually the trip involved a fifteen-hour flight from Chicago to Beijing or Shanghai, a three-hour layover, then another three-and-a-half-hour flight to Kunming, finally ending with a three-hour car trip from Kunming to the smaller city where they lived. To say we arrived exhausted would be an understatement.

However, this time the grueling trip became even longer because the best flights we could find to China directed us from Chicago to Germany and Germany to China. Plus, on the way home, we would fly east from Beijing to Washington DC. Then we would catch a connecting flight west to Chicago. This meant we would fly completely around the world and then some.

The long hike through the Frankfort airport seemed to fit the theme of this trip: a long journey made even longer. The children of Israel faced a long journey from Egypt to the Promised Land, but we will see in this chapter that the grueling trip was even longer than it needed to be.

SETTING THE SCENE

In chapter 3, we left Rebekah at the point of arriving from her home to start a new life with Isaac. Rebekah became mother to Jacob, who fathered twelve sons—including Joseph. Because of family discord and jealousy, Joseph's brothers sold him into slavery in Egypt. However, God eventually moved Joseph from the lowly rank of a slave to the second-highest position in the land, from which Joseph used his divinely revealed insight to save the region from starvation during a seven-year famine.

Joseph's family of origin also suffered from the famine and eventually joined him in Egypt around 1876 BC. What may have begun as a temporary move ended up as a 430-year stay (see Exodus 12:40), during which

Jacob's clan of seventy people "multiplied and grew exceedingly strong, so that the land was filled with them" (Exodus 1:7).

Of course, during these years, the ruling powers of Egypt changed many times. Bible historians surmise that the pharaoh in charge during Joseph's lifetime was one of the Hyksos pharaohs—foreign rulers from modern-day Syria and Iraq. Centuries later, Ahmose I defeated the Hyksos dynasty and reigned 1539–1515 BC. As a true Egyptian, he did not want to continue the policies of the despised foreign rulers who had shown favor to Jacob's clan.[4] So during the sixteenth century BC, Ahmose I forced the children of Israel into slavery to build the cities of Pithom and Ramses as supply centers. However, the more Ahmose oppressed them, "the more they multiplied and the more they spread abroad" (v. 12).

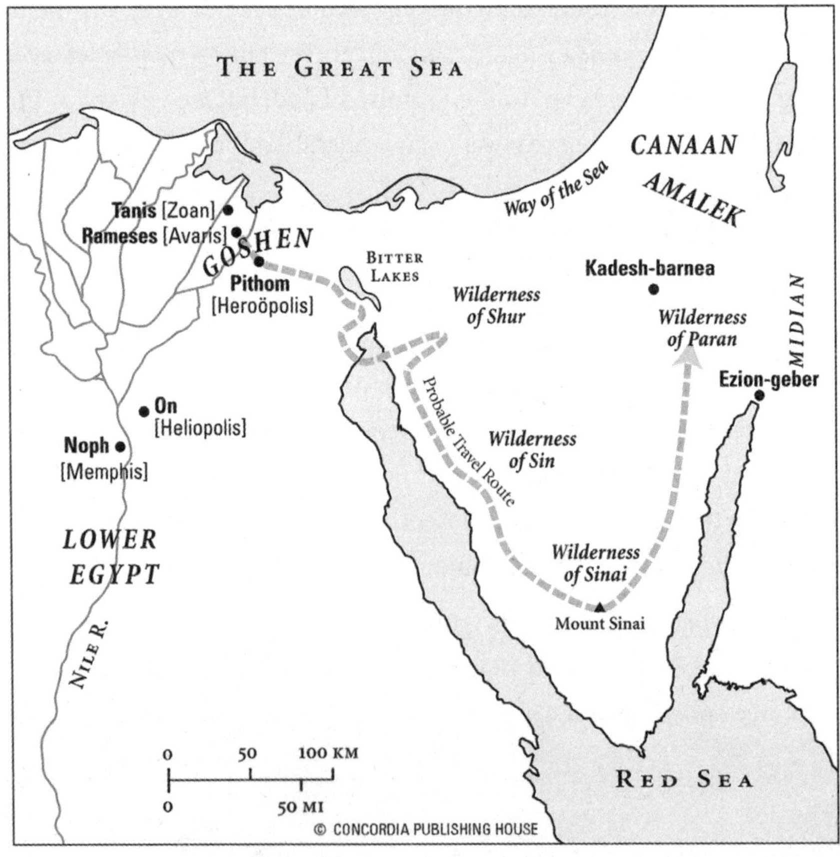

After many years of slavery, God called Moses to free His people. He sent Moses to a new pharaoh named Thutmose III in 1446 BC to demand that the ruler let the Israelites go free.[5] But Thutmose III was no dummy. He didn't want to lose the free labor he had in the Israelite slaves. He refused to let them go. It took ten plagues in the land, including the deaths of all firstborn sons in Egypt, including firstborn sons of female slaves and even cattle, before Thutmose finally let the people go.

After 430 years in Egypt—of which almost 100 were spent in slavery—the children of Israel began their journey to the Promised Land.

THE JOURNEY

When I imagine participating in the exodus, this is what I see: When we left Egypt, we rejoiced. No more brickmaking! No more enduring the whips of the taskmasters! Every day the Lord guided us with a pillar of cloud. At night, the pillar transformed into an amazing display of fire. We followed the pillar. We followed Moses. We followed the Lord to freedom.

But, the pillar of cloud led us to Pi-hahiroth—a place that made no sense. A great sea stretched ahead of us. On one side lay a range of craggy rocks. On the other some outposts of Egypt. The situation turned from bad to worse when we heard the clatter of six hundred chariots behind us. Surely Pharaoh and his army would seize us here in this desolate desert. We felt like two million defenseless targets with nowhere to go.

Moses tried to reassure us, "Don't be afraid. The Lord will fight for you. You will never see these Egyptians again." I almost laughed at these words.

But then the pillar of cloud moved from the front of the horde of people to the back, hiding my view of the Egyptians. Moses lifted up his staff, and a powerful wind began to blow. The sea actually began to part! Tall walls of water stood up, and a path through the water opened before our eyes!

Moses urged the people at the front to begin walking on this miraculous path. As evening fell, God lit our way with the shining cloud as we marched through the night. As I neared the edge of the sea, the roar of the water drowned out the rattle of the chariots. When I set foot on the path, I expected a muddy mess, but my feet were on dry ground! I felt the spray from the miraculous waves on my face and sensed a faint taste of salt on my lips. I looked around in amazement. How could walls of water as tall as buildings exist?

God made a way where there was no way. Every step took us closer to safety. Each footstep brought us closer to freedom.

ON THE MAP: THE RED SEA

Exodus 13:18 tells us, "But God led the people around by the way of the wilderness toward the Red Sea." The name *Red Sea* comes from the Hebrew phrase *yam suph,* which should be translated Sea of Reeds, indicating a body of water surrounded by an abundance of reeds. However, the Septuagint (the Greek version of the Old Testament) translated the phrase into Greek words meaning Red Sea, and the name stuck. We don't know exactly where the Israelites crossed the sea, but it could have been at what is now the Gulf of Agaba, the Gulf of Suez, or the Bitter Lakes.*

* *See* NIV Cultural Backgrounds Study Bible, *"Exodus 13:18: The Red Sea."*

JOURNEY FROM SLAVERY TO FREEDOM

When God called Moses, He told him, "Say therefore to the people of Israel, 'I am the Lord, and I will bring you out from under the burdens of the Egyptians, and I will deliver you from slavery to them, and I will redeem you with an outstretched arm and with great acts of judgment'" (Exodus 6:6). God promised to free the people of Israel from slavery and redeem them.

This journey to freedom not only sums up the central point of the book of Exodus, but it pictures the message of the entire Bible. It explains the journey of our own lives. Without Christ, we all live as slaves—slaves to sin. In John 8:34, Jesus said, "Truly, truly, I say to you, everyone who practices sin is a slave to sin." Ever since the fall, our natural inclination leads us to serve our sinful desires and Satan's promptings. We may think life without God gives us freedom from His restricting Law, but in reality, our sinful desires rule over us. Greed binds us to material possessions and the work it takes to get them. Pride enslaves us to keeping up appearances to gain the approval of others.

But thanks be to God! He made a way to freedom! Martin Luther wrote, "He has redeemed me from sin, from the devil, from death, and from all evil. For before I did not have a Lord or King, but was captive under the devil's power, condemned to death, stuck in sin and blindness."* Just as God sent Moses to lead the people to freedom in the Promised Land, so the Father sent His Son, Jesus, to redeem us and lead us to a life of freedom in eternity with Him.

* *Large Catechism, Part 2, Paragraph 27.*

OUR LIFE JOURNEY MAY FOLLOW A ZIGZAG PATH

The Israelites' journey to freedom began with God calling Moses. The Sunday School stories of Moses demanding Pharaoh let the people go and the dramatic account of the parting of the Red Sea might cause us to think that Moses' path to greatness followed a linear, never-faltering road to becoming the leader of Israel. But a closer reading of Exodus shows that Moses' route was a zigzag path.

When Moses was born, it seemed he was destined for great things. His mother knew right away that "he was a fine child" (Exodus 2:2). (Of course, doesn't every mother feel that way about her new baby?) She could not bear to see her beautiful baby boy destroyed by Pharaoh's edict to throw every Hebrew boy into the Nile (see Exodus 1:22), so she hid him in a basket among the reeds of the river. Ironically, that same pharaoh's daughter found Moses and adopted him. He grew up in Pharaoh's palace. Who could doubt that this little Hebrew boy, raised as an Egyptian prince, would grow up to be an influential Israelite leader?

However, Moses' life took a detour from greatness at age 40 when he saw the oppression of his people taking place and took action by killing an Egyptian who beat up one of his fellow Hebrews (see Acts 7:23–30). When Moses realized that others knew what he had done, he fled to the desert of Midian. There he married Zipporah and started a family. They lived as humble shepherds in the wilderness. Did Moses' life look like stupendous success at that point? Not so much.

Forty years later, Moses' life took another zigzag. One day in the wilderness, God called to Moses from a burning bush. He had an important job for this unassuming shepherd: to free the people of Israel. Moses objected, saying that he could not possibly speak for the people before Pharaoh: "Oh, my Lord, I am not eloquent, either in the past or since You have spoken to Your servant, but I am slow of speech and of tongue" (Exodus 4:10). But God insisted he was the man for the job. To calm Moses' urgent fears, God said He would send Moses' brother, Aaron, with him.

We know the rest of the story. Moses confronted Pharaoh. Pharaoh eventually freed two million Israelites. Moses led them to the Promised Land, and 3,500 years later, we still talk about the boy who grew up to free the people of Israel.

From the time we are young children, people ask us, "What do you want to be when you grow up?" How did you answer? Did you have grand ideas of becoming a movie star or an astronaut? Did you want a flashy profession like a firefighter or a politician?

Even now, you might ask yourself similar questions because you've entered a new phase of your journey. You've had your career. You've accomplished your professional goals. Now, in retirement, you find yourself asking, "What next?"

The world tells you that you should have all these details figured out. That by your first year in college, you should know what you want to do for the rest of your career. That by the time your coworkers throw your retirement party, you should have volunteer positions lined up and your new free time scheduled.

Sometimes things work out that way. But often the road to a meaningful vocation seems to zig and zag in unpredictable and frustrating ways.

We might even feel like Moses, who experienced a couple of life-altering detours. We don't get into the college that will lead to our dream profession. We don't make the cut as a firefighter. The job we've always wanted is phased out.

Or our current situation feels like years in the wilderness because we don't know exactly what God wants us to do with our time, our talents, our lives. We try multiple jobs or volunteer positions, but nothing seems to fit our gifts or personalities. We ask, "Have I missed God's calling? Does He even want to use me?"

It's possible that Moses asked similar questions during his time in the Midian desert. But we can see from his life that a path to God's calling may not follow a straight road. Even if we start out confident and capable, circumstances or mistakes may lead us into a wilderness for a time. However, God can transform wrong turns and missteps into a highway that displays His glory. While in the wilderness, God shaped Moses into an instrument He could use. Moses started out as someone who rescued one Hebrew slave with his own strength in an unholy act, but he became a leader who helped free two million Hebrew slaves through the strength of Yahweh.

As a child, I dreamed of becoming a teacher. I even played teacher with my dolls as students! When I entered college, I did so with a plan of becoming a professor of piano. But after I earned a master's degree in piano performance, we moved to Montana. No openings for piano professors there. Later, we moved to the Chicago area, where there are dozens of colleges and universities. But by then we had two children, and I decided to prioritize my family over my career. For fifteen years, as I homeschooled my kids, I sometimes felt that I lived in a vocational wilderness far from my dreams. When my kids graduated from our homeschool and went to college, perhaps I could have pursued teaching positions at colleges, but by then God had called me to a new way to use my teaching skills: speaking and writing about His Word. Like Moses, my vocational wilderness time humbled me and shaped me into something new, and my life road ended up going in a direction I never expected.

If you feel your life is on one long bypass, one long alternate route that leads to nowhere, take heart in Moses' story. **God can use all the zigs and zags your path has taken to bring you to the destination He had planned all along.** He will use every life circumstance to shape your soul. Just because you have landed in a wilderness, it doesn't mean you're in the wrong place.

BAPTIZED INTO MOSES

In 1 Corinthians, the apostle Paul compares the Israelites passing through the Red Sea to Baptism. He writes, "For I do not want you to be unaware, brothers, that our fathers were all under the cloud, and all passed through the sea, and all were baptized into Moses in the cloud and in the sea (1 Corinthians 10:1–2). Author R. Reed Lessing writes, "In Holy Baptism, we experience a personal exodus. Like Pharaoh long ago, our old self drowns and dies. And, baptized into Christ, like Israel long ago, we are freed from bondage and are now heading for our own heavenly promised land."* Let us thank God for washing away our sins in the sea of His grace and leading us on our personal exodus to freedom in Him.

* *Lessing,* Deliver Us, *11.*

SOMETIMES THE LONG WAY IS THE BEST WAY

Anyone tracing the route of the Israelites as they left Egypt would want to run down and give them a GPS programmed with the shortest route to Canaan because they were obviously not going the right way! If you look at the map of the area (such as the one on page 64), you can clearly see that to get from Egypt to Canaan, you travel northeast. But the pillar of cloud led them south! Did the pillar of cloud need a map update?

No. God purposefully chose this path for the Israelites. Exodus 13:17–18 tells us, "When Pharaoh let the people go, God did not lead them by way of the land of the Philistines, although that was near. For God said, 'Lest the people change their minds when they see war and return to Egypt.' But God led the people around by the way of the wilderness toward the Red Sea."

A direct trade route from Egypt to Canaan ran along the coast of the Mediterranean Sea. If God had led the people of Israel along this 150-mile route, called the Way of the Sea, they could have arrived at the Promised Land in about ten days![6] Why didn't God program the pillar of cloud to lead them that way? Because along that route, they would have encountered Egyptian outposts and Palestinian settlements (see *TLSB*, note on Exodus 13:17). War would have been inevitable. The people who had lived as slaves for so long were not prepared for battle.

On that extra-long journey my husband and I made to China, we had even more trip extensions. When the day we were to begin our trek home arrived, we got up at 3:00 a.m. to travel by car from our daughter's house to the airport in the big city of Kunming. We arrived in time to check our baggage and find our gate. From there we would fly to Beijing, change planes, fly to Washington DC, and change planes again for the final flight to Chicago. The first leg of the trip went well. We arrived at the airport with plenty of time to spare and found seats at the gate. We rejoiced when we saw the plane already parked at the Jetway. But when our boarding time came and went, we wondered what was causing the delay. After thirty minutes of waiting, the gate attendants posted a sign on the check-in desk. Our fellow passengers got up and read the sign in Chinese characters, nodded their heads, and sighed. I got up and read the English portion of the sign, which said, "Flight 397 is delayed because ___________________." Evidently the Chinese gate workers did not know enough English to write an explanation we could understand. We knew our flight was delayed, but we didn't know why.

I spotted another passenger who looked like he might be from an English-speaking country. I asked, "Do you understand what is happening?" It turned out he was British but was traveling with an English-speaking Chinese man who explained that Beijing was experiencing severe thunderstorms. We couldn't fly there until the storms passed.

Our longest trip from China became even longer with that three-hour weather delay. But the delay was for our safety.

We may also experience delays in life, but I always want the quickest route. "Grant me success, Lord. And if You please, place me on the fast track!" But the Lord knows when delays keep us safe. He knows when the long route will bring greater success.

The pillar of cloud led the Israelites from Rameses southeast to Succoth (see Exodus 12:37), then further northeast to Etham at the edge of the wilderness (see Exodus 13:20). Anyone who knew this area was aware that this was not the way to Canaan, but God's next instructions would have left them scratching their heads even more. God told Moses, "Tell the people of Israel to turn back and encamp in front of Pi-hahiroth, between Migdol and the sea, in front of Baal-zephon; you shall encamp facing it, by the sea" (Exodus 14:2). Go back? Toward Egypt? Moses may have wanted to argue, "Um, not to question Your plan, Lord, but did You know this campsite puts us in a suboptimal position with the salt marshes of Pi-hahiroth on one side, mountains on the other, and the sea in front of us?" Still, Moses obeyed God.

Not long after the Israelites had set up camp, Pharaoh's six hundred chariots arrived. Now the Israelites truly faced an impossible situation. They had no way of escape—or so they thought. Why did God lead the Israelites to this roadblock?

Two reasons.

First, God wanted to demonstrate His power to Pharaoh and the Egyptians. When Moses first approached Pharaoh to give him Yahweh's message, "Let my people go," Pharaoh said, "Who is the LORD, that I should obey His voice and let Israel go?" (Exodus 5:2). But after God parted a large body of water and drowned the Egyptian army, Pharaoh could no longer deny the awesome might of Yahweh.

Second, God wanted to bolster the faith of His people. Seeing their oppressors so triumphantly defeated most certainly increased their trust in Him. Exodus 14:31 says, "Israel saw the great power that the LORD used against the Egyptians, so the people feared the LORD, and they believed in the LORD and in His servant Moses."

At times, you might find yourself in impossible situations too. The house you own and can afford no longer fits your growing family. You get the perfect job that makes the ends of your budget meet, but you can't find a daycare worker for your son that will allow you to take the position. You might be tempted to respond like the Israelites did when they saw the Egyptian chariots closing in on them—with fear. But you can also listen to the words of Moses like the Israelites did: "Fear not, stand firm, and see the salvation of the LORD" (Exodus 14:13).

Fear not. Don't let panic and anxiety rule your heart. Hang on to God's promises. Remember His trustworthy character and His strong arm to save.

Stand firm. Resist the temptation to run away or dash back to slavery to sin or to other gods. Stay where God has placed you: in the middle of His caring hand.

See the salvation of the Lord. While you stand firm, watch and see how God works everything out. You may not see your enemies piling up in drowned heaps on the seashore, but you may find God's care in an unexpected check in the mail or in the kindness of a friend who offers to babysit your children.

God's divine direction may direct us to the long way and even allow us to encounter seemingly hopeless circumstances in order to increase our trust in His will for us, just as He did for the Israelites. God is much more interested in transforming our hearts than He is in paving an easy road to success. **Along the paths that look like detours and dead ends, God molds us to look more like His Son.**

REMEMBER TO PACK: YOUR VALUES

When you pack for your life journey, you need to take your key values. This seems like an obvious principle when making decisions, yet we often get side-tracked by what the world says we need. Instead, take time to investigate what God determines is important: values like love, relationships, righteousness, and wisdom. Then assess what means most to you: Is it your relationship with God? Your family? Compassion for others? Make a list and keep it visible when faced with choices. It will make decisions easier as you recognize that you value time with your family more than an optional work conference or peace with your neighbor more than winning an argument with them. Pack your values and carry them with you.

TRAVELING WITH GOD IS THE GOAL OF OUR JOURNEY

Do you remember what happened when Moses came down from Mount Sinai after receiving the Ten Commandments? Did he find the people of Israel fervently praising Yahweh for saving them from slavery and from Pharaoh's army? No, Moses found the people worshiping a counterfeit god—a calf fashioned out of gold jewelry.

Of course, God had witnessed this and informed Moses, "I have seen this people, and behold, it is a stiff-necked people. Now therefore let Me alone, that My wrath may burn hot against them and I may consume them, in order that I may make a great nation of you" (Exodus 32:9–10). The stiff-necked Israelites had exhausted Yahweh's patience.

But Moses interceded for the people and begged God to remember His promise to Abraham. God relented. He would not destroy the people. He would even lead them to the Promised Land—"a land flowing with milk and honey" (Exodus 33:3a). There was just one catch. God declared, "I will not go up among you, lest I consume you on the way, for you are a stiff-necked people" (v. 3b).

At this news, I might have said, "Well, as long as I don't have to go back to slavery, I can accept that. If I can still dwell in the land of milk and honey, I can live with it." But "when the people heard this *disastrous* word, they mourned" (v. 4, emphasis added). Although the people had momentarily forgotten the greatness of Yahweh and had chosen a poor substitute, they realized what a disaster their lives would be if God wasn't with them. Author R. Reed Lessing writes in his book *Deliver Us* that "God's decision not to accompany Israel into the Promised Land isn't a minor adjustment to the plan. *It's the end of everything.*"[7]

So Moses again interceded on behalf of the people. Listen in on his conversation with God:

> "Now therefore, if I have found favor in Your sight, please show me now Your ways, that I may know You in order to find favor in Your sight. Consider too that this nation is Your people." And He said, "My presence will go with you, and I will give you rest." And he said to Him, "If Your presence will not go with me, do not bring us up from here. For how shall it be known that I have found favor in Your sight, I and Your people? Is it not in Your going with us, so that we

> are distinct, I and Your people, from every other people on the face of the earth?" (vv. 13–16)

Can you hear the desperation in Moses' voice? He didn't want to continue the journey without God.

QUESTIONS FOR CLARITY

God includes the account of the exodus in His Word to guide us through our own life journeys and assure us of His might and provision. As we move from slavery in sin to freedom in Christ, let's consider our path by asking ourselves some questions.

- **Have you experienced a life-altering detour?** Do you sometimes feel stuck in a vocational wilderness? How does Moses' zigzag path to become the leader of God's people encourage you? How have past detours helped you understand your vocation as a baptized child of God wherever you roam?
- **Why does God sometimes lead us the long way around or allow us to set up camp in impossible situations?** How does the Israelites' journey demonstrate that God prioritizes our transformation rather than a speedy trip to a particular destination? How can this perspective help you when your path seems to veer to the longest route possible?
- **What is the goal of your life journey?** Take some time to name some of your dreams and aspirations. How do these compare to the objective of traveling with God? When setting new goals and making life decisions, how can you take into account that walking with God is our ultimate purpose? How does that change your goals? How can you remember that He constantly walks with you?

This makes me think of our trips to China. We saw some amazing sights, including the Great Wall and the Forbidden City in Beijing. We explored the Stone Forest and the Nine Dragons Waterfalls in the Yunnan province. But we didn't take long journeys to China to visit tourist attractions. We went to be with our daughter and her family.

Like my trips to China, like the Israelites' trek to the Promised Land, our life journeys have a purpose. Some might think the point of our time on earth is to amass great fortunes, accumulate valuable possessions, reach a certain rank at work, or check off items on our bucket lists. But the whole goal of our lives is to walk with God. Without Him, our journeys become meaningless.

May we, like Moses, value God's presence more than anything else. Praise God that all who believe in Jesus' saving work of dying on the cross to forgive our sins never need to go a day without His presence. The Holy Spirit comes to us in our Baptism, in the moment of faith, and our very bodies become tabernacles of God. **Let's remember that wherever the road takes us, as long as we walk with Jesus, we can revel in the journey.**

DIVINE DIRECTIONS: LED BY HIS STEADFAST LOVE

When Moses and the children of Israel crossed the Red Sea and witnessed the destruction of the Egyptian army, they celebrated with a song that began, "I will sing to the Lord, for He has triumphed gloriously; the horse and his rider He has thrown into the sea" (Exodus 15:1). Can you imagine two million voices singing that chorus at the top of their lungs?

In the middle of that song comes a beautiful verse:

> You have led in Your steadfast love the people whom You have redeemed;
>
> You have guided them by Your strength to Your holy abode. (v. 13)

God leads us by His steadfast love—a love strong enough to sacrifice His own Son in order to release us from the chains of sin and death. A love wise enough to know when the long way is the best way. A love deep enough to never abandon us even when we turn from Him toward the shiny idols our culture worships.

So when you're wondering which road to take, skeptical of the path you're on, or wishing you could take a faster route to your dreams, remember this: God leads you in His unfailing love. He guides you with the same power and purpose that made a path through a sea. He will provide divine directions for you too—a path to His holy abode.

* * * * *

Yahweh, the great I AM,
sometimes my life feels like
one long detour in the desert,
a path to nowhere,
an extended stay by a sea of fear and doubt.
But Yahweh, You tell me,
"Sometimes the long way is the best way.
The wilderness can shape character.
Sit back and watch Me work."
O great I AM, even here,
help me anticipate Your victory,
lead me to freedom,
show me Your glory,
and with every step, remind me of Your presence.
In Jesus' name. Amen.

CHAPTER 5

NAOMI AND RUTH

A Road to Grace

TIMELINE

Abram (Abraham)	ca. 2100 BC
Hagar	ca. 2081 BC
Rebekah	ca. 2026 BC
Moses and the exodus	1446 BC
Naomi and Ruth	ca. 1100 BC

My husband and I climbed on the tram in Vienna, Austria, ready to see the city's sights. I eagerly anticipated our visit to this city because many of my favorite classical composers had lived and worked there. I couldn't wait to tour the homes of Mozart, Beethoven, and Brahms! But first, we needed to see the famous St. Stephen's Cathedral with its multicolored tile roof.

Although I had a guidebook and a map of Vienna, we weren't sure if we were taking the best route to get to the cathedral. I decided to gather my courage and try speaking German—a language I had (sort of) learned in high school. I tentatively tapped a kind-looking, middle-aged woman on the shoulder and hoped I had the correct words as I asked, "*Wo ist Stephansplatz?*"

Fortunately, I had the correct German words. Unfortunately, the woman assumed I knew German much better than I did and started to give me detailed directions *auf Deutch*. I tried to follow along, but I only comprehended about half of what she said.

When she noticed the blank expression on my face, she smiled. Then, with a wave of her hand, she said, *Komm mit mir*. "Come with me."

We got off the tram at the next stop, closely following the woman as she turned left, then right, then left again. Abruptly, we found ourselves in a broad city square. The woman pointed up to the towering cathedral, with its patterned tiles gleaming in the sunshine. She said, *Das ist Dom St. Stephan*.

Danke, I feebly said, wishing I remembered more German vocabulary so I could express my gratitude to this woman who had gone out of her way to guide us. She smiled and said, *Bitte schön*, and went on her way.

In the book of Ruth, we read about Naomi returning to her homeland after losing her husband and two sons. You would think she would want company on this lonely journey. But instead of telling her daughters-in-law, *Komm mit mir*, she urged them to return to their native country, Moab. We know that the account doesn't end there. One of the young women refuses to leave her mother-in-law's side. Their journey encourages all of us that even when the road we travel on appears dark and lonely, we never truly travel alone.

SETTING THE SCENE

In chapter 4, we watched Moses lead the Israelites through the wilderness to the Promised Land. Joshua took over leadership of the Israelites from Moses in 1406 BC and led the nation into Canaan, beginning the fight to overtake the land. After the death of Joshua, the people of

Israel periodically abandoned the one true God and served the false god Baal (see Judges 2:11–12). During this period, which lasted until the coronation of King Saul in 1048 BC, God raised up judges like Deborah (see Judges 4–5) and Gideon (see Judges 6–8) to lead the people when the Israelites cried out to Him for mercy. But after the people received His help, they inevitably abandoned the one true God again. The last sentence of the book of Judges sums up this period: "In those days there was no king in Israel. Everyone did what was right in his own eyes" (Judges 21:25).

It is in this rather faithless time period that God reveals to us a familiar story of faith: the account of Naomi and Ruth. The book of Ruth begins with these words: "In the days when the judges ruled there was a famine in the land, and a man of Bethlehem in Judah went to sojourn in the country of Moab, he and his wife and his two sons" (Ruth 1:1). The famine must have been severe for Elimelech, Naomi, and their sons, Mahlon and Chilion, since it caused them to leave their homeland. Perhaps they chose Moab because it was just east of Bethlehem on the other side of the Dead Sea. They lived there for ten years (see v. 4). During that time, Elimelech died, and Naomi's sons married Moabite women named Orpah and Ruth. Then disaster struck again. Both sons died, and Naomi faced life alone in a foreign country. Could things get any worse?

Finally, Naomi heard some good news that led her on a journey back to Bethlehem. We don't know the exact path of her journey, but if she traveled around the northern end of the Dead Sea, she probably traveled thirty to fifty miles. Because of the steep and rugged terrain, the trip could have taken seven to ten days.[8]

Naomi began the trip with both of her daughters-in-law, but the plan for the journey changed along the way.

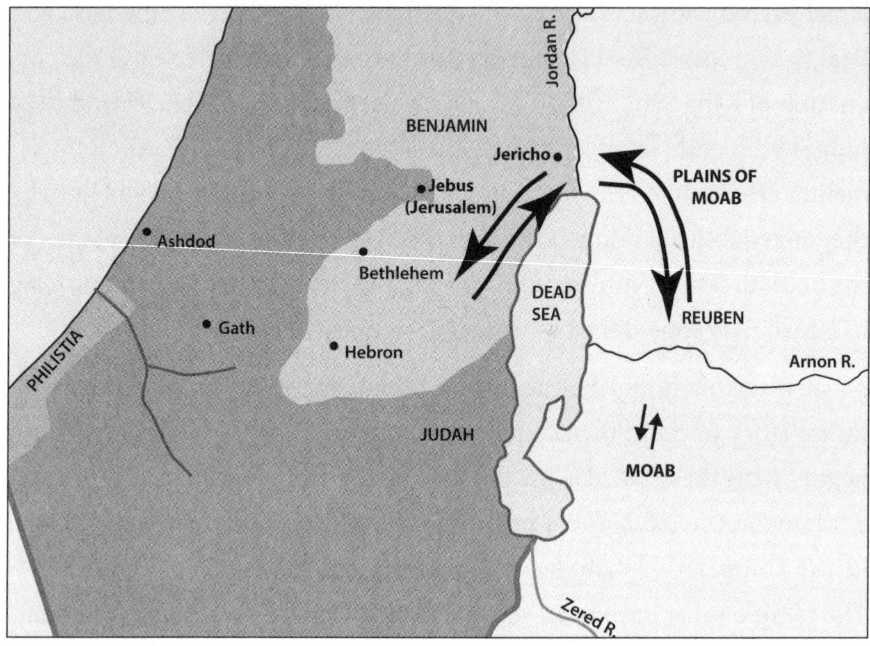

MAP © ISTOCK.COM / PETER HERMESFURIAN

THE JOURNEY

Here's how I imagine the scene: Three women trudged up the steep path, carefully picking their steps on the arid mountainside. The barren landscape was a fitting setting for their situation as sorrow seemed to follow them wherever they went. In almost unbelievable circumstances, Naomi, Orpah, and Ruth had all lost their husbands.

Naomi's family had come to the foreign country of Moab to escape starvation, but her husband and sons had died anyway. When she heard that Yahweh had again blessed Israel with harvests, she knew she needed to return to her hometown of Bethlehem. Widowhood would never be easy, but perhaps life would be more manageable among her own people.

As they walked, Naomi stopped on the nearly vertical road to catch her breath. She turned and looked at the two younger women behind her. When she had told her daughters-in-law that she planned to leave

Moab, they volunteered to go with her, and she gratefully accepted their company.

But at that moment, as she made her way home, Naomi knew she couldn't ask them to leave their own homeland. She had experienced living in a foreign culture away from the support of her family. She couldn't ask Orpah and Ruth to suffer that same separation and hardship. Especially because they probably would have been shunned and persecuted in Israel as foreigners.

Naomi took a deep breath and said, "Orpah and Ruth, I think it best that you return home. I pray that Yahweh will repay your compassion to me by giving you comfort and security in the homes of new husbands."

Every eye filled with tears as she hugged them. The two younger women protested, "No, we want to come with you." But Naomi insisted, "Turn back, my daughters. I'm too old to remarry. I have no more sons to become your husbands. The situation is bitter for us all, but you can find new spouses. I feel the Lord's hand has gone against me."

More tears flowed as Orpah agreed to go back home. But Ruth persisted, "You can't stop me from coming with you. I will go where you go. I will live where you live. Your God will be my God. May Yahweh punish me if anything but death parts us."

Naomi gave in to Ruth's determination. As she wiped the tears from her cheeks, she grabbed Ruth's hand and gave it a squeeze. With a grateful smile, she faced the upward path again. Hand in hand, the two women continued their journey.

RETURN TRIP TO THE GRACE OF GOD

When Naomi left Israel, she escaped the physical famine plaguing her homeland, but she entered a new kind of famine—a spiritual one. The people of Moab did not worship Yahweh; they bowed down to many false gods and even used human sacrifice in worship to their principal god, Chemosh.[9] Naomi may have been able to feed her body in Moab, but it would have starved her spirit. For ten years, her family had no access to the tabernacle or the spoken word of Yahweh.

ON THE MAP: MOAB

Elimelech and his family moved to Moab. What do we know about this country?

- The nation was made up of descendants of the man Moab, the son born from an incestuous relationship between Lot and his older daughter (see Genesis 19:34–38).
- Moabites had a reputation for promiscuity. When the Israelites journeyed through Moab on the way to the Promised Land, the Moabites enticed them to worship their false gods through sexual relations with the women of Moab (Numbers 25:1–13).
- God declared Moab an enemy of Israel because they did not provide "bread and with water on the way" (Deuteronomy 23:4) when Israel left Egypt.

Naomi's lack of spiritual nourishment showed up in the choices her family made. While in Moab, both of her sons took Moabite wives. While God did not specifically forbid marriage to Moabites until much later in Israel's history (see Nehemiah 13:23–27), God clearly forbid intermarriage with foreigners in Deuteronomy 7:1–4 because "they would turn away your sons from following Me, to serve other gods" (v. 4). That Mahlon and Chilion married Orpah and Ruth in spite of God's command could indicate the family's spiritual decline.[10]

The word *return* is a significant word in Ruth 1. In fact, the Hebrew word for return, *šûḇ*, translated as "return" or "go," appears twelve times in this chapter. The word indicates a literal turning back or returning. But the Old Testament also uses it in a spiritual sense—to turn back to God.

Psalm 78:34 translates *šûḇ* as *repent*: "They repented [*šûḇ*] and sought God earnestly." So *šûḇ* not only describes Naomi's geographical return to the land of Judah "but a spiritual one as well. She is returning to Yahweh and still clings to Him by faith."[11]

We all need to return to God. From the moment our heavenly Father gives us earthly life, we experience a separation from Him because of our sinful nature inherited from Adam and Eve. Because Jesus has bridged the gap between God's holiness and our sinfulness, we can confidently walk back into the Father's embrace. When the Holy Spirit creates faith in our hearts through the Word and Sacraments, we return to God.

But even then, we may take side trips away from the heart of God. Like Naomi, we may think we'll find more nourishment in another place. We fear danger and decide taking matters into our own hands will solve the issue. We pack up our problems and take them to seminars and self-help sessions hoping to find answers for our empty hearts.

I think of that European trip my husband and I took in the days before cell phones and GPS. Guidebook in hand, we traversed not only Vienna but London, Rome, and Paris. Although we sometimes successfully navigated these foreign cities, one wrong turn on narrow streets could have led us far from where we wanted to go. This may also happen in our spiritual journeys. Although we may always intend to travel toward God, at times, one misstep may take us in the opposite direction. Thankfully, the account of Naomi encourages us that even when we have settled in a land far from God, we can always return to Him.

When our wrong choices have led us into a territory far from God, let's rejoice that God continuously welcomes us back—back to His land of grace. We can rest our weary heads on His mercy.

Our life journey is one long return trip to the grace of God.

WIDOWHOOD

Whenever a woman loses her husband, she experiences a gargantuan loss. But while widows today may have monetary support through life insurance, inheritance, or their own source of income, women in Bible times faced great financial lack. They rarely had means to support themselves, so when their spouse died, they turned to their sons. If a woman had no sons, she might need to turn to prostitution or sell herself into slavery.*

We see God's heart for widows throughout Scripture. Old Testament laws provided protections for women facing widowhood. New Testament writers gave instruction to care for women who had lost their husbands. The words of Psalm 146:9 demonstrate God's care for widows: "The Lord watches over the sojourners; He upholds the widow and the fatherless."

* *See* NKJV Cultural Backgrounds Study Bible: Bringing to Life the Ancient World of Scripture, *note on Ruth 1:3.*

GET OUT OF MOAB

When my husband and I asked for directions in Vienna, we asked how to find St. Stephen's Cathedral—a magnificent church built to worship almighty God. I think Ruth's plea to travel with Naomi also indicated a desire to worship the one true God. She said, "Do not urge me to leave you or to return from following you. For where you go I will go, and where you lodge I will lodge. Your people shall be my people, and your God my God. Where you die I will die, and there will I be buried. May the Lord do so to me and more also if anything but death parts me from you" (Ruth 1:16–17). Ruth used the covenant name of God, Yahweh, when she said, "May the Lord do so to me." Ruth abandoned Moab with all its false gods to willingly follow the one true God.

Although Elimelech and Naomi left Judah and the opportunity to worship God at His tabernacle, Ruth must have witnessed them practicing their faith at some level. Maybe they practiced a weekly Sabbath. Perhaps they continued to celebrate Passover. When she heard stories of how Yahweh rescued His people from Pharaoh, she discovered a powerful yet caring God so very different from the demanding, vengeful Chemosh. Ruth probably understood the likelihood of prejudice against her in Judah, yet she willingly took the journey that led her closer to the one true God. She wanted to get out of Moab.

Does it feel like we currently live in Moab? Just as the Moabites prayed to many false gods, our culture worships the idols of money, success, and fame. People revere sports icons and celebrity idols. It seems a lot of the people in our world accept any god except Jesus.

We may also have personal Moabs, where our hearts journey away from our loving Father. I know I have spent time in Moab when I have worshiped the god of accomplishment that made me sacrifice time with my family. I have turned to the god of self-fulfillment. I have spent time at the altar of busyness.

What is your personal Moab? Have you journeyed to the nation of financial gain, working long hours to the exclusion of studying God's Word? Have you traveled to the land of risky relationships, spending time with a person who made you feel good but led you away from God? Have you taken a trip to harmful habits with routines and practices that led you in the wrong direction?

At first, our time in Moab seems to feed our empty souls. In adopting the attitudes of Moab, we find acceptance and approval when we fit into the culture around us. **But when we get a glimpse of Yahweh, we clearly see that all the false gods we've found in that country are only cheap imitations of the one true God.** We remember Moab can never truly feel like home.

Naomi knew she needed to return home to Bethlehem. And Ruth, though she was raised in Moab, understood her true home lay ahead in Judah, where she could worship Yahweh. Let's all adopt Ruth's attitude. Let's get out of Moab. When faced with decisions, consider these questions: "Which choices lead us back to Moab, with its worldly practices and harmful habits? Which routes guide us toward our loving heavenly Father?"

Leave behind Moab and journey to the heart of the one true God.

GOD REDEEMS OUR BITTER ROADS

When we first meet Naomi, we see a bitter, grieving woman. The loss of her husband and both of her sons sent her into an emotional chasm. Twice Naomi described her life as bitter. When she urged Orpah and Ruth to go back to Moab, she told them, "It is exceedingly bitter to me for your sake that the hand of the Lord has gone out against me" (v. 13). Our hearts go out to Naomi. She lost the three most important people in her life.

Naomi again described herself as bitter when she arrived in Bethlehem and the local women asked, "Is this Naomi?" Of course, ten years can do a number on anyone's face, but even more than gravity, grief had changed this Bethlehem native. Naomi told her neighbors, "Do not call me Naomi; call me Mara, for the Almighty has dealt very bitterly with me" (v. 20). Her deep depression caused her to renounce the name *Naomi*, which means "pleasant," and adopt *Mara*, which means "bitter." She recognized the power of God by calling Him *Shaddai*—the almighty God—but felt His power had only brought her harm, not good.

If we live long enough, most of us will experience seasons of loss. We may walk a road filled with grief, financial disaster, or a dire medical diagnosis. And like Naomi, we may question why God has led us down these painful highways.

Thankfully, Naomi's journey didn't end on that bitter road. Her story assures us that God can *redeem* all of our painful paths. In fact, Naomi's bitter road took a U-turn right after she called herself Mara, when the writer of the book of Ruth tells us, "And they came to Bethlehem at the beginning of barley harvest" (v. 22). The beginning of harvest signaled a change from insufficiency to plenty, from emptiness to fullness.

As soon as the two women arrived in Bethlehem, faithful Ruth didn't wait to work for their survival. She told Naomi, "Let me go to the field and glean among the ears of grain after him in whose sight I shall find favor" (Ruth 2:2). You see, the Lord commanded the Israelites not to reap their fields to the edge or pick up every last grape in their vineyards. He instructed them to instead leave gleanings and fallen grapes "for the poor and for the sojourner" (Leviticus 19:10). Not every landowner observed this law though. Ruth needed to find someone who would show her favor and allow her to pick up grains of barley in their field.

Ruth's saga continued: "So she set out and went and gleaned in the field after the reapers, and she happened to come to the part of the field belonging to Boaz, who was of the clan of Elimelech" (Ruth 2:3). She *happened* to come to the field of Boaz. Was this a coincidence? Not at all. God's hand constantly worked behind the scenes to direct Ruth to this kind and worthy man.

As Ruth began working in the field, Boaz visited the harvesting process and noticed her. After asking the identity of this young woman, he discovered she was the Moabite woman who had returned with Naomi. Boaz had heard about all she had done for Naomi and decided to help not only by giving Ruth permission to glean his field but by telling her to closely follow the women tying the grain in sheaves so she could have the first chance at any grain that falls. He even told his workers to purposely pull out some grain from the bundles and leave it for the Moabite woman.

BREAD AND WINE

Boaz went above and beyond to help Ruth. In addition to allowing her to glean his field, he asked Ruth to join him at the midday meal: "Come here and eat some bread and dip your morsel in the wine" (Ruth 2:14). Inviting a foreigner to join the master's table would have been very unusual. But Boaz foreshadowed Christ in this act. Jesus invites all of us, who started out as foreigners in His kingdom, to partake of bread and wine—His body and blood—in His Holy Supper.

When Ruth returned to Naomi after working all day, she brought home an ephah (about twenty-two liters!) of barley. Finally, we hear Naomi speak something positive! She said, "Blessed be the man who took notice of you" (v. 19). And when Naomi discovered the identity of the man, she informed Ruth, "The man is a close relative of ours, one of our redeemers" (v. 20). Did you see it? That word *redeemer*?

God provided for widows through the laws of the kinsman-redeemer—someone who could help a relative in dire need through buying back, or redeeming, a family property sold because of extreme poverty. Perhaps Elimelech had sold the harvest rights to his property when the family moved to Moab. When Naomi heard that Ruth had gleaned Boaz's field, hope began to grow in her heart. Perhaps this kinsman-redeemer could help them.

Ruth continued to work in Boaz's fields for the seven weeks of the barley harvest.[12] Let's fast-forward to the end of the harvest and the beginning of the threshing and winnowing of the crop. On the day that Boaz would thresh his grain, Naomi came up with a plan. She gave Ruth detailed instructions: Wash and anoint yourself. Go to the threshing floor. Observe Boaz as he winnows his grain. Watch him as he eats and drinks his evening meal. Then Naomi told her, "When he lies down, observe the place where he lies. Then go and uncover his feet and lie down, and he will tell you what to do" (Ruth 3:4). You might wonder, "Uncover his feet?

Lie down on a pile of grain?" We might not envision this as the perfect marriage proposal, but that is basically what Ruth's actions indicated.

KINSMAN-REDEEMER AND LEVIRATE LAWS

God provided for widows through two sets of laws: kinsman-redeemer and levirate laws.

- **Kinsman-Redeemer:** The Hebrew term *go'el* indicated a kinsman-redeemer—a close relative who had the responsibility to help a family member in need or in danger. Responsibilities of the *go'el* included buying back land (see Leviticus 25:25) and redeeming a relative that had gone so far into debt that he had sold himself as a slave (see vv. 47–55).
- **Levir:** If an Israelite man died without having a child, the practice of levirate marriage came into effect. God instructed the *levir*—brother of the deceased—to marry the widow and conceive a child in the name of his brother, therefore providing for the widow and carrying on the lineage of the dead man (see Deuteronomy 25:5–10).

Although Scripture does not insist on the *go'el* taking on the duties of the *levir* as Boaz did, it may be true that these duties were combined more often than we see in Scripture.*

* *See Edward A. Engelbrecht, ed.,* Lutheran Bible Companion, vol. 1, Introduction and Old Testament *(Concordia Publishing House, 2014), 262.*

The suspense builds. What would Boaz do?

Boaz noticed Ruth and told her that he intended to do all that she had asked. But just when we think the fairy-tale ending is near, we find a wrinkle in the plot. Boaz told Ruth he must first check with another man who was a closer relative and therefore had the first rights to redeem her and Naomi's property.

The next morning, Boaz went to the city gate where all important business took place. He approached the nearer relative and told him about Naomi's field. This unnamed man responded eagerly to the opportunity to purchase the property but declined when he heard that marrying Ruth was part of the deal.

Why did he decline? Because he knew that if he purchased the land but had a son with Ruth, he would never recoup the cost of the property; Ruth's son would inherit it. He was not willing to make the sacrifice. But Boaz was. Because of the kinsman-redeemer and levirate laws, the field he purchased could belong to Ruth's son in the name of her first husband, Mahlon. Yet Boaz sacrificed the price of the land to obtain a future for Ruth and Naomi.

So, we come to the happily-ever-after ending: "Boaz took Ruth, and she became his wife. And he went in to her, and the Lord gave her conception, and she bore a son. Then the women said to Naomi, 'Blessed be the Lord, who has not left you this day without a redeemer, and may His name be renowned in Israel!'" (Ruth 4:13–14).

REMEMBER TO PACK: HOPE AND LAMENT

When we find our journey is strewn with sorrow, let's continually carry hope. Like King David, let's remind our hearts, "For God alone, O my soul, wait in silence, for my hope is from Him" (Psalm 62:5).

That doesn't mean we also need to carry a Pollyanna attitude. In the same psalm, David cries out, "How long will all of you attack a man to batter him, like a leaning wall, a tottering fence?" (v. 3). David feels faint and wobbly from constant attack. He doesn't hide his weakness but prays a prayer of lament. When we walk bitter roads, God does not expect us to simply ignore the pain and paste a smile on our faces. He invites us to pour out our "heart before Him" (v. 8). Then, as we empty our hearts of sorrow, we can ask the Holy Spirit to fill them with hope in the God of goodness and grace.

God transformed Naomi's story of bitter emptiness into joyful fullness. The four short chapters of Ruth offer a microcosm of the whole saga of the Bible.[13] Just as Naomi and Ruth had nothing but emptiness and poverty before Boaz redeemed them, we were spiritually empty and poor until Christ came to redeem us. The final words of the book of Ruth point to the Redeemer of the world through, of all things, a genealogy! Ruth 4:21–22 says, "Salmon fathered Boaz, Boaz fathered Obed, Obed fathered Jesse, and Jesse fathered David." The Gospel of Matthew continues the lineage with this: "The book of the genealogy of Jesus Christ, the son of David, the son of Abraham" (Matthew 1:1). Boaz redeemed Ruth, and they became the ancestors of Jesus, who would *redeem them*. Naomi never could have guessed that her bitter road would lead to the salvation of the world.

What bitter roads have you traveled on? The loss of a loved one? The loss of a marriage? The loss of financial security? You may feel that the road God has placed you on has nothing but rocks and ruts. But the end of Naomi's journey reassures us that God's redeeming power can repave any bumpy road into a smooth highway leading to eternal abundance. He cares about our individual losses, and His divine directions can transform them into lavish blessings for all.

God can redeem any bitter, painful road.

DIVINE DIRECTIONS: EVEN ON ROADS WE DO NOT CHOOSE

When my husband and I traveled to Vienna and a local resident said, *Komm mit mir*, she led us exactly where we wanted to go, to St. Stephen's Cathedral. But life often leads us on roads we do not choose. God's Word encourages us that God goes with us no matter what. Isaiah 42:16 says,

> And I will lead the blind
> in a way that they do not know,
> in paths that they have not known
> I will guide them.

I will turn the darkness before them into light,
the rough places into level ground.
These are the things I do,
and I do not forsake them.

God promises to go with us on paths we've never traveled before or would never have chosen. He will transform darkness to light, potholes and bumps to smooth pavement. Sometimes our paths become filled with disappointment, disease, or death. But God can redeem those broken roads. I have witnessed this. A woman who sought out an abortion before she knew Christ now directs a Christian home for women with crisis pregnancies. Another woman who came through a cancer diagnosis and treatment now counsels newly diagnosed cancer patients.

QUESTIONS FOR CLARITY

- **What does it mean to you that our whole life journey is one long return trip to the grace of God?** When have you journeyed away from God? How has He called you back? How has repentance and a return to God's grace changed your life? When you make decisions, do you examine each choice as a turn toward God or a step away?
- **When have you traveled to Moab?** Do you have one foot in that culture right now? When faced with decisions, do you consider which options may represent Moab and which keep in line with worship of the one true God?
- **Have you traveled on a long, bitter road?** How has God redeemed the road for you? How can His work of redemption continue through you as you help others on a similar road? If you find yourself on a painful path right now, how can you remind yourself that God cares about your situation and continues to work behind the scenes to bring good out of every problem?

Ruth and Naomi's trip from Moab to Bethlehem demonstrates that even when we have traveled far from God, we can always return to His grace. Personal Moabs seem to promise safety and fulfillment, but deep inside, we know that a journey to the one true God is the only thing that will satisfy us. Naomi's story demonstrates that God can redeem all of our painful paths.

Remember that God continues to walk beside you to bring you to a heavenly place, even when your road seems impossible to trek. He graciously beckons, *Komm mit mir.*

* * * * *

El Shaddai, God Almighty,
when I wander away from You, help me remember that
You constantly invite me to return to
Your grace.
When I spend too much time in Moab,
remind me that
I will never find fulfillment there.
When my road seems filled with bitterness,
tell me again that
You can redeem all the pain for my good.
El Shaddai, God Almighty,
though my road seems
strewn with disappointment and death,
I eagerly watch as Your power repaves it with
Your grace and goodness.
In Jesus' name. Amen.

CHAPTER 6

JONAH

Detour Before Destination

TIMELINE

Abram (Abraham)	ca. 2100 BC
Hagar	ca. 2081 BC
Rebekah	ca. 2026 BC
Moses and the exodus	1446 BC
Naomi and Ruth	ca. 1100 BC
Jonah	780 BC

If it's Monday, this must be Rome.

During the decade I homeschooled our kids, my husband and I had sometimes wistfully expressed a desire to take them on an extraordinary field trip to some of the places they had studied in history class. When 2002 arrived, it seemed like the perfect time to go. Due to the events of September 11, 2001, US travelers hesitated to fly, and airlines dropped their fares. Plus, at 16 and 13, Anna and Nathaniel were old enough to appreciate the experience and still young enough to consent to being seen with their parents.

We signed up for a European bus tour (or "luxury motor coach tour" as the brochures described it) and looked forward to seeing the major sights of Europe, including Brussels, Innsbruck, Venice, Florence, Nice, and Paris. But we were especially excited to visit the ancient city of Rome. On the day we arrived in that great Italian city, our luxury motorcoach took us to the Vatican for a tour of the Sistine Chapel and St. Peter's Basilica. Craning our heads back in the Sistine Chapel, we stared at Michelangelo's incredible ceiling. The sheer size of St. Peter's astounded us. How appropriate that we felt miniscule in this sanctuary dedicated to our great God!

After lunch, everyone in our tour group had the freedom to sightsee on their own. We figured out how to use public transportation to get to the Roman Forum. Then we went on to a tour of the Colosseum. Next, we walked to the Pantheon, built in AD 120. We kept walking and saw the Italian Parliament building and Trevi Fountain. After walking about seven miles that day, our feet started complaining. With our trusty bus map, we found out how to get back to our hotel. When the correct bus pulled into the terminal, we boarded it, walked to the back of the vehicle, and breathed a sigh of relief at the chance to sit for the fifteen-minute ride to our destination.

However, halfway up the hill to the hotel, policemen stopped all traffic and forced all vehicles to turn around. Animated Italian conversations erupted all over the bus. Finally, someone explained to us in English, "Your President Bush has come to Rome today. They have blocked off the road for his motorcade." The driver returned the bus to the terminal. Then he tried to complete its route only to be turned back once more. After riding on the bus for an hour, we ended up exactly where we had started.

While the bus sat at the terminal for what seemed like ages, we debated what to do. Surely, after this long delay, the bus would now be allowed to continue its route so we could reach our hotel, right? But if it turned around again, should we get off and walk the rest of the way to our hotel? When the bus started up again, we hadn't made any decisions, and when we saw that it was taking a different road up the hill, we hoped this route would have more success. But again, officials forced the bus to turn around when it neared the top of the hill.

Suddenly, Nathaniel stood up and got off the bus! As the door shut behind him, the bus driver hit the gas pedal, and we yelled in a panic, "Stop!" We pushed open the doors and quickly exited. For a few tense seconds, we had pictured being separated from our thirteen-year-old son in a foreign city of 2.5 million people. As we watched the bus lumber down the hill, we had a few words with him. But our teenager just shrugged it off and said, "Someone needed to take action." After more than two hours on that bus, he had had enough.

We trudged up the hill, and after walking another three miles, we finally reached our hotel and collapsed in our beds.

Nathaniel knew he didn't want to go where the bus was headed, so he decided to get off. In this chapter, we will learn about Jonah, who decided he didn't like the route God had planned for his life, so he took off in the opposite direction.

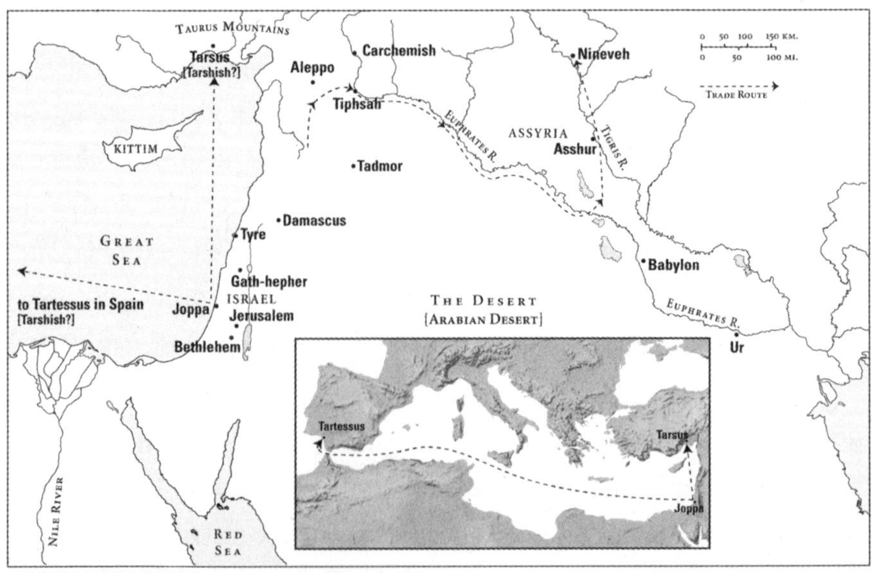

SETTING THE SCENE

In chapter 5, we learned about Ruth and Naomi, who lived in the time of the judges in the eleventh century BC. God worked in Ruth's life to make her the great-grandmother of King David. After David died, his son Solomon took the throne and ruled over a united kingdom. But when Solomon died, the kingdom split. Solomon's son Rehoboam reigned over the Southern Kingdom of Judah, and Jeroboam I ruled over the Northern Kingdom of Israel.

About 140 years later, another King Jeroboam governed the Northern Kingdom, and a prophet named Jonah spoke to him: "[Jeroboam] restored the border of Israel from Lebo-hamath as far as the Sea of the Arabah, according to the word of the Lord, the God of Israel, which He spoke by His servant Jonah the son of Amittai, the prophet, who was from Gath-hepher" (2 Kings 14:25). During Jeroboam II's reign from 793 to 753 BC, Israel retook land that other nations had captured, and Israel prospered. All this success was a gift from God and announced by Jonah.

But God did not limit Jonah's prophetic ministry to Israel. The Lord had big plans for Jonah. He sent him to the great city of Nineveh. Growing up, I had always enjoyed the account of Jonah and the great fish whenever it turned up in our Sunday School lessons. But I never understood why Jonah didn't want to go to Nineveh. Did Nineveh have too many bugs? Did it not have good ice cream? What was the big deal about this place?

Well, it turns out that Nineveh was about five hundred miles from Jonah's hometown. As a kid, I could have traveled five hundred miles in about ten hours in my dad's trusty Buick, but in Jonah's day, the journey would have required about a month of traveling through searing deserts—without air conditioning! Perhaps Jonah didn't want to make this grueling journey.

However, even more than not jumping at a chance to ride a camel for five hundred miles, Jonah probably balked at the idea of visiting

Nineveh because it was located in Assyria, one of Israel's archenemies. King Jeroboam II had just reclaimed some of Israel's land from this brutal nation. Maybe some of Jonah's relatives had experienced violence or loss of property at the hand of the Assyrians. Asking Jonah to preach to Ninevites may have been like asking a Polish citizen to share a word of God's forgiveness to German Nazis after World War II. Jonah gratefully accepted mercy for himself as part of God's chosen people but not for these Gentile enemies. So when Yahweh said, "Go to Nineveh," he decided to hop on a ship going in the opposite direction.

ON THE MAP: NINEVEH

Archaeologists have found the ruins of the ancient city of Nineveh on the Tigris River, near the modern-day city of Mosul, Iraq. In Jonah's day, Nineveh was an impressive city, "three days' journey in breadth" (Jonah 3:3). Before and after Jonah's time, Assyrians oppressed the nation of Israel. However, during Jonah's day, Assyrian power had dwindled through military defeats, diplomatic failures, famine, and domestic rebellions.* This may help explain why the people of Nineveh responded so quickly to Jonah's message of doom.

* *See* Archaeological Study Bible *(Zondervan, 2005), 1469.*

THE JOURNEY

This is how I imagine the scene: "Where are you from? What is your occupation? Who are your people? Why is this happening to us?" The sailors simultaneously hurled questions at him, shouting above the noise of the storm.

Through the roar of the wind and the pelting of the rain, Jonah yelled back, "I am a Hebrew, and I fear the Lord, the God of heaven, who made the sea and the dry land."

At this the sailors all took a step back, and not because of the pitching of the ship! Their raised eyebrows and gaping mouths spoke their astonishment even more than their next question: "What have you done?" Although these hardy sailors worshiped their own deities, they could scarcely believe someone would defy the supreme God—the one who created the world.

What had he done, indeed. Just days ago, God had given Jonah a new message. But He wanted him to go to Nineveh, to speak to Assyrians! He knew he should have obeyed the Lord, but he just couldn't make himself travel five hundred miles east to speak to enemies of Israel. So, Jonah went west.

At Joppa, a port on the Mediterranean Sea, he got on the first ship he could find. When he heard this ship was headed to Tarshish, he thought, "Good. That's about as far away from Nineveh as I can get. Maybe I won't hear God's voice there."

But he should have known better. Not long after the ship left port, the captain came down to Jonah's quarters and woke him from a nap. Over the roar of a storm and violent rolling of the ship, the captain yelled, "Get up and pray to your God! Perhaps He will listen to you so we won't die in this storm!" That's when Jonah realized that he couldn't escape Yahweh. God had orchestrated this storm.

On deck, the sailors had decided to cast lots to discover who was responsible for their frightening situation. And, of course, when a sailor reached into the bag of lots, he pulled out Jonah's marker. Yahweh controlled the wind, the rain, the sea, and this silly game.

Even as the rain whipped the sailors' faces, they shouted again, "Jonah, what have you done?"

He didn't want to tell them the whole story and admit to foolishness in trying to escape the God who created the depths of the sea and the force of the wind. But when the boat pitched even more wildly, Jonah acknowledged that he didn't want these innocent men to die because of his stupidity. He shouted, "Pick me up and hurl me into the sea, then the sea will quiet down for you, for I know it's because of me that this great tempest has come upon you."

To their credit, the men tried to avoid that option, knowing it almost certainly meant his death. They rowed with all their might, trying to reach land, but the waves only intensified. Finally, they lost hope and threw Jonah into the sea, asking the great God not to punish them for this deed.

Immediately, the sea became as calm as tea in a teacup.

But even without the storm, the prophet couldn't swim to shore. Just when he had given up all hope of survival, a great fish surfaced and swallowed him.

The God of creation used—of all things—a fish to save his life.

A GREAT FISH

And the LORD appointed a great fish to swallow up Jonah. And Jonah was in the belly of the fish three days and three nights. (Jonah 1:17)

Ancient peoples used the term *great fish* for any large sea creature. They did not distinguish between ocean mammals and fish as modern science does.* Also, the Hebrew word for belly is not precise and may indicate any large body cavity. It is possible that Jonah may have endured three days in the oral cavity of a whale. As a mammal, a whale would need to come to the surface for air, therefore also providing oxygen for Jonah.**

* *See* TLSB, *note on Jonah 1:17.*
** *See* Archaeological Study Bible, *1474.*

CASTING LOTS

When the storm on the Mediterranean Sea raged, the sailors said, "Come, let us cast lots, that we may know on whose account this evil has come upon us" (Jonah 1:7). What did the casting of lots entail?

The Hebrew word *gôrāl* refers to "pebbles used for systematically making decisions" or "small stones used for casting lots." We don't know the exact method the sailors used, but casting lots generally involved each person putting a pebble, clay or wooden cube, or some other identifiable item in a container. The container was likely shaken up and down. The first marker to fly out indicated the one the gods had "chosen."* Or someone might handpick an item out of the container.**

The casting of lots in Jonah's account indicates one more way God took charge of the circumstances. He even controlled the game of chance to indicate that Jonah was the reason for the storm.

* *See* NKJV Cultural Backgrounds Study Bible, *note on Jonah 1:7.*
** *See* Archaeological Study Bible, *744.*

DIVINE INTERRUPTIONS

The book of Jonah begins this way: "Now the word of the LORD came to Jonah the son of Amittai, saying, 'Arise, go to Nineveh, that great city, and call out against it, for their evil has come up before Me'" (Jonah 1:1–2).

We don't know what Jonah was doing when the word of the Lord came to him. We do know from 2 Kings that the prophet had spoken to King Jeroboam II, a ruler who reigned during a period of prosperity. Some commentators surmise that Jonah had ample personal resources if he could afford passage on a ship to Tarshish. Some experts even note that the original Hebrew could be translated to mean Jonah hired out the entire ship![14] So we might picture Jonah living a comfortable life in Gath-hepher, enjoying the position of a favored prophet of the king. He did not want God to interrupt his cushy life with an arduous journey.

We also don't know how the word of the Lord came to Jonah. Did God speak in an audible voice? Did Yahweh tap on Jonah's heart? Did He deliver the message through someone else? We all want to receive the word of the Lord. I think of times when I desperately desired a specific direction from God. I cried out, "Please, God, show me which way to go. Speak to me. Write in the sky." But I wonder what I would have done if God had rented out a billboard along a highway and wrote,

> Dear Sharla,
> I want you to go to Papua New Guinea to share My Good News.
> Thanks,
> God

I probably would have acted a lot like Jonah. I would have tried going north instead of south.

Usually, when I seek God's direction for my life, I really mean, "Lord, please approve my plans" or "I have two good and favorable options, God. Which one will give me the most success and satisfaction?" Like Jonah, I don't want God to break into my comfortable life and inconvenience my schedule. I don't want Him to detour the usual bus route that is my life.

At times, God's divine deviations have involved big changes to my plans, like moving to western Montana instead of the eastern United States. But often His redirections simply involve changing my daily schedule to accommodate a friend's urgent need. It may mean I don't get all the items on my to-do list checked off, but from my reaction, you might think God had asked me to go to Nineveh.

Like Jonah, we may balk at God's instructions because we have already decided our way is best. The Bible tells us about God's ways: "For My thoughts are not your thoughts, neither are your ways My ways, declares the Lord" (Isaiah 55:8). Maybe you pray a lot like me: "O Lord, it would be so much more convenient if Your thoughts and plans matched mine!" Are we willing to let God redirect our lives? Are we ready to obey the Lord if He tells us to get off the bus?

REMEMBER TO PACK: A TEACHABLE HEART

Perhaps the most important item to pack when determining God's route for our lives is a teachable heart. Psalm 25:9 tells us, "He leads the humble in what is right, and teaches the humble His way." You'll notice it doesn't say, "God reveals His will to those who insist their way is right" or "The Lord directs those who stubbornly demand their own route." Instead, our loving Father gently guides those who take His hand, admit they don't know the best way to go, and allow Him to lead step by step.

Reading on in Isaiah 55, we learn why we can say yes to God's interruptions:

> For as the heavens are higher than the earth,
> so are My ways higher than your ways
> and My thoughts than your thoughts. (v. 9)

Although I am sure my plans are the best, God's divine directions are even better. When we realize this, we can follow His route for our lives.

Learning to live in God's will means allowing God to interrupt our plans with His.

GOING IN THE OPPOSITE DIRECTION

Our family kept going in the wrong direction when we rode that bus in Rome. Jonah, too, went the wrong way. Why did he insist on this contrary route? We can't be sure, but Jonah 4 gives us more clues.

ON THE MAP: TARSHISH

Scholars don't know the exact location of Tarshish. It could mean Tarsus in Asia Minor or Tartessus, a Phoenician city in Spain.* Tarshish is mentioned in 1 Kings 10:22, which describes King Solomon's great wealth: "For the king had a fleet of ships of Tarshish at sea with the fleet of Hiram. Once every three years the fleet of ships of Tarshish used to come bringing gold, silver, ivory, apes, and peacocks." Some commentators take this to mean it took three years for ships to go from Israel to Tarshish.** Or it could mean that they made the journey only once every three years. In any case, we can see that Tarshish was a great distance in the opposite direction of Nineveh.

* *See the map in* TLSB *at the start of the book of Jonah.*
** *See* NKJV Cultural Backgrounds Study Bible, *note on Jonah 1:3.*

You see, after Jonah spent three days and three nights inside the great fish, it regurgitated him on land. Once he was back on dry land, Jonah finally decided to obey the Lord. Yahweh again gave Jonah the mission to go to Nineveh, and this time Jonah went. When he arrived, he spent days walking through the city and calling out, "Yet forty days, and Nineveh shall be overthrown!" (Jonah 3:4). And a miracle even greater than surviving three days and three nights in the belly of a great fish happened: the people of Nineveh responded to Jonah's sermon. They believed God and repented. Everyone in the city, from the king to the least important citizen, fasted and put on sackcloth as a sign of their sorrow over sin.

You would think Jonah would rejoice that his preaching had had such a marvelous effect. But instead, "it displeased Jonah exceedingly, and he was angry" (Jonah 4:1). Jonah expressed his anger to God:

> O Lord, is not this what I said when I was yet in my country? That is why I made haste to flee to Tarshish; for I knew that You are a gracious God and merciful, slow to anger and abounding in steadfast love, and relenting from disaster. (v. 2)

In other words, Jonah said, "Doggone it, God! I knew this would happen! I had a feeling that because You are a loving and gracious God, You would show mercy to these good-for-nothing, evil, treacherous people of Nineveh."

Jonah didn't want to have anything to do with the brutal Assyrians who had overtaken his land in the past. Although he was a Jewish prophet, he seemed to misunderstand that it was Israel's role to produce the Messiah and be a light to the world, and he didn't want to share God's message of mercy to Gentiles. He might have feared that if God showed the Assyrians mercy, their power would again increase.[15]

You might have noticed something ironic. Jonah describes God as "slow to anger." That phrase definitely does not describe Jonah. God noticed this too. He asked Jonah, "Do you do well to be angry?" (v. 4). The Hebrew could also be translated, "Are you right to be angry?"

Jonah must have thought his anger was justified because he continued to pout. He walked out of the city and set up a shelter made of branches in a spot where he could see the city. Perhaps he thought, "Just in case God decides to do away with these scoundrels, I want to see the fire and brimstone."

That little hut of sticks helped cool Jonah a bit, but in a land where temperatures can soar to 110 degrees, he most likely sweated through his tunic. God again demonstrated His merciful character by appointing a shady plant to grow for Jonah. However, Jonah's glee in the shade didn't last long. The next day, God sent a worm to attack the plant, which wilted. Next, God sent a scorching east wind. Jonah became so uncomfortable that he said, "It is better for me to die than to live" (v. 8).

God again addressed Jonah's anger, saying, "Do you do well to be angry for the plant?" (v. 9a). You might think Jonah would begin to realize his response was over the top, but he insisted, "Yes, I do well to be angry, angry enough to die" (v. 9b). God then attempted to point out the error in

Jonah's thinking. Jonah grieved the loss of shade over his head, but God grieved the 120,000 people who lived in Nineveh.

I want to laugh at Jonah, but I have exhibited similar anger at times. I had anger when I didn't get the job I thought I deserved. When someone else got the speaking engagement I wanted. When I was hurrying to an appointment and hit every red light. Do you notice a pattern? Like Jonah, my anger was based on my selfish desires.

Like Jonah, anger may send me in the opposite way I should go. Maybe not to literal Tarshish, but to a destination far from God's will for me. Indignation may send me to the land of pouting instead of obedience. Anger may lead me to bitterness instead of forgiveness. Resentment may pull me toward demanding my rights instead of accepting God's will.

But we shouldn't always stuff down our anger. David's psalms demonstrate that we can open up to God with all our messy feelings. We can take them to Him, and He will help us figure them out. When the Lord asks, "Do you do well to be angry?" what if we heard that question as an invitation to examine our feelings and what's behind them. If we don't do that, we may make decisions based solely on our rage instead of seeking God's will. We might take the job two states over just to get away from the friend who hurt us. We might decide to date someone just to prove our worth to someone who jilted us.

Instead of letting anger pull us in the wrong direction, let's talk out our outrage with God and ask Him for divine directions to the right path.

WE CAN'T RUN FROM GOD

When our son bolted from the bus in Rome, do you think we thought, "That's okay—let him find his own way; we'll probably catch up with him later"? Of course not! We loved him too much to let him go off on his own. In the same way, God loved Jonah too much to let him run away without trying to bring him back. Yahweh could have allowed Jonah to sail off to Tarshish to start a new life, but He didn't give up on him. Instead, Yahweh orchestrated events to bring Jonah back to the right path.

Let's read Jonah 1:3 again:

> But Jonah rose to flee to Tarshish from the presence of the Lord. He went down to Joppa and found a ship going to Tarshish. So he paid the fare and went down into it, to go with them to Tarshish, away from the presence of the Lord.

Jonah tried to flee. The Hebrew verb used for Jonah "fleeing" (*bārah*, Jonah 1:3, 10; 4:2) suggests a desperate attempt to get away from God by any means possible. Of course, it is impossible for him to conceal his escape from God. But Jonah tried to sneak away as if he thought, "If I sneak out of Israel quickly and quietly, God won't notice, and I won't have to face Him."

It seems that Jonah forgot the words of Psalm 139:7, 9–10:

> Where shall I go from Your Spirit?
> Or where shall I flee from Your presence? . . .
> If I take the wings of the morning
> and dwell in the uttermost parts of the sea,
> even there Your hand shall lead me,
> and Your right hand shall hold me.

Foolish Jonah tried to make a getaway to "the uttermost parts of the sea," but he couldn't escape God's reach or His love for him. God saw Jonah slipping away and immediately set things in motion to bring him back. Throughout the book of Jonah, we see God's control over everything in creation. He "hurled a great wind upon the sea" (Jonah 1:4) and "appointed a great fish to swallow up Jonah" (v. 17). The Lord "spoke to the fish, and it vomited Jonah out upon the dry land" (Jonah 2:10). He "appointed a plant" to shade Jonah (4:6) and then "appointed a worm that attacked the plant, so that it withered" (v. 7).

FACT OR FICTION?

Is the account of Jonah and the great fish fact or fiction? There aren't many other accounts in the Bible that get challenged more often than Jonah's journey.

However, there are scientific and historical facts that support this almost unbelievable story of a man surviving three days and three nights inside a sea creature. An article written in 1927 tells of the swallowing capabilities of sperm whales. The bodies of whole octopuses and the sixteen-foot skeleton of a shark—both much larger than a man—have been found inside sperm whales. Plus, history documents two instances when a man survived being swallowed by a sperm whale: Marshall Jenkins in 1771 and James Bartley in 1891.*

But the best reason to accept the book of Jonah as true is that Jesus talks about the book as a historical fact, not a parable. In Matthew 12:41, He says, "The men of Nineveh will rise up at the judgment with this generation and condemn it, for they repented at the preaching of Jonah, and behold, something greater than Jonah is here."

Although the tale seems like a giant fish story, God can do anything—even save a man from drowning by appointing a sea creature to swallow him and then ordering it to deposit him back on land.

* *Engelbrecht,* Lutheran Bible Companion, *1:917–18.*

Over and over we see that God took control of everything from a great fish to a tiny worm, from the wind to the sun to the vegetation. Why did God go to so much trouble? To give Jonah a second chance. To lead him to repentance. To bring a wayward son back to His love and mercy.

What grace for Jonah—and for us! Jonah's journey shows us that if we try to run in the opposite direction of God's plan for our lives, the

Lord will orchestrate events to draw us back to Him. **Even when we try to escape God's gaze, He will still pursue us.**

DIVINE DIRECTIONS: DESIGNED TO BRING US BACK TO HIM

We may think we have total control over where the bus of life will take us. And if it starts going in the opposite direction we want to go, we may desperately want to jump off.

But the account of Jonah assures us that when God interrupts our plans, it's because He has something else in mind for us. When our sin sends us in the wrong direction, the Lord will pursue us. When we try to run away, God will appoint a fish or a worm, a layoff or an illness to get our attention. **He does it all to bring us back to Him.**

QUESTIONS FOR CLARITY

Jonah's story can give us guidance for our lives. Use these questions for discerning your next steps.

- **How do you respond to God's divine interruptions?** Do you give your plans priority over God's? How can you remember the privilege of being part of God's mission, even when it seems inconvenient?
- **Do anger or other emotions often propel your decisions?** What would it look like to pause and talk out your emotions with God before reacting? Which emotions propel your choices most often? Fear? Jealousy? Feelings of inadequacy?
- **When have you tried to run from God? What did that look like?** Do you see God's control of the universe as a good thing or something that gets in the way of what you want? What is your response to the truth that when you try to run away, God will orchestrate events to draw you back to Him?

* * * * *

O Lord,
forgive me
when I attempt to flee Your plan,
when I try to run in the opposite direction of Your grace.
At times, I've ridden on ships of anger,
resentment,
stubbornness,
pride.
Thank You
for loving me enough to pursue me,
for arranging events just to bring me back to You,
for never abandoning me in the sea of my mistakes.
In Jesus' name. Amen.

CHAPTER 7

THE MAGI

Excursion to the King

TIMELINE

Abram (Abraham)	ca. 2100 BC
Hagar	ca. 2081 BC
Rebekah	ca. 2026 BC
Moses and the exodus	1446 BC
Naomi and Ruth	ca. 1100 BC
Jonah	780 BC
The Magi	ca. 1–2 BC

My eyes bounced back and forth from the printout of driving directions I clutched in my right hand to the road ahead. I gripped the steering wheel as I drove to the restaurant where I would speak at a women's luncheon. Stress often gripped my heart when I needed to find my way to a new place, follow the printed directions, pay attention to street signs, and avoid hitting anything.

I was grateful for the detailed route I had discovered on the internet, but my gratitude fizzled when the directions told me to turn left at the next stop sign and into a cornfield!

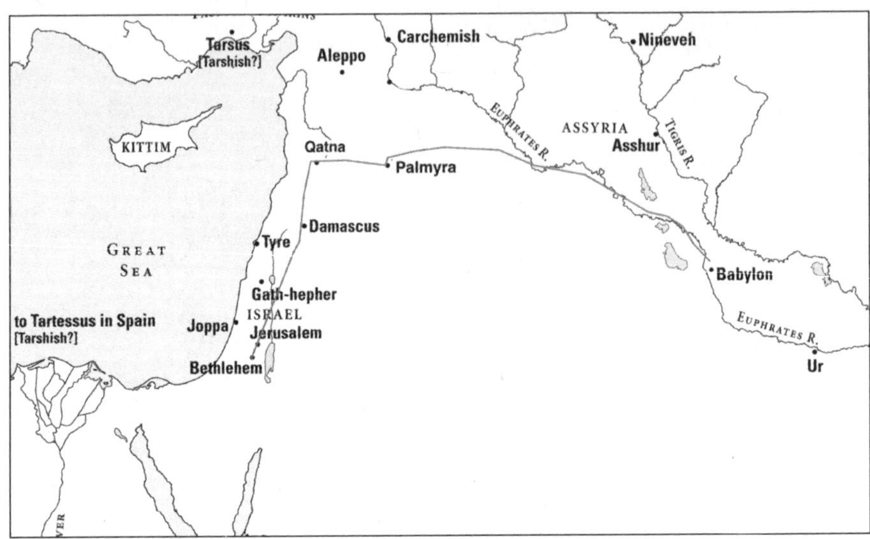

MAP © CONCORDIA PUBLISHING HOUSE

Obviously, the computer program that generated my route did not have all the current information.

Do you, like me, remember times before the internet, when we relied on actual paper maps to plot our routes? We needed to buy the correct map, figure out where we were on the map, find our destination, then plot the best route to get there. Online navigation sites changed all that. We were grateful for optimized routes and time estimations—until they told us to turn into cornfields!

Now we program our destination into our smartphone, and the app tells us when and where to turn. We don't need to think about the best route or which roads to avoid. The app plans the path, and we're guided by our phone, which is guided by satellites in the sky.

The Magi had their own GPS in the sky guiding their journey. Long before satellites and smartphones, long before algorithms that computed the most efficient route and multicolored maps depicting seemingly endless paved roads, the Magi followed a sign in the sky to Bethlehem, where they would worship a new king.

SETTING THE SCENE

In chapter 6, we explored the journey of Jonah, who had clear direction from the Lord but decided to go the other way. In the end, though, he traveled from Israel to Nineveh—from west to east. In this chapter, we will look at a journey in the opposite direction. The Magi left from the East, making their way westward to Judea.

Most of us sing or hear the songs "As with Gladness Men of Old" (*LSB* 397) and "We Three Kings of Orient Are" during Epiphany. At Christmastime, we see nativity sets with figures in colorful robes clutching treasure chests and elaborate jars. We may think we already know everything about this account. But can we learn something new about the Magi if we look a little closer? Can we glean information about our own journeys as we study theirs?

The Gospel writer Matthew tells us their story:

> Now after Jesus was born in Bethlehem of Judea in the days of Herod the king, behold, wise men from the east came to Jerusalem, saying, "Where is He who has been born king of the Jews? For we saw His star when it rose and have come to worship Him." (Matthew 2:1–2)

The Greek word translated *wise men* in the English Standard Version of the Bible is *magos*, which is where we get the term *Magi*. The term originally referred to a priestly group in Persia that practiced astrology, astronomy, and dream interpretation. Rulers often sought out Magi for their wisdom and made them important advisers in their courts.

We don't know exactly what Matthew meant by "the east," but if these Magi did indeed come from Babylon in Persia, they might have been influenced by the prophet Daniel. Daniel 5:11 tells us that Daniel was the "chief of the magicians, enchanters, Chaldeans, and astrologers." In other words, he took charge of the Magi in Babylon.[16]

The Magi in Matthew's account may have consulted Daniel's writings and prophecies some six hundred years later when they saw the unusual star. The information they found indicated a new, important ruler had been born in Judea. So, they headed west.

I had always assumed that the unusual star guided them all the way from the East to Jerusalem, but a closer look at the grammar in the Greek of the phrase "We saw His star when it rose" implies that when they told Herod about the star, it wasn't visible.[17] They saw the star when they were still at their homes in the East. Their studies informed them that this astronomical phenomenon was a sign that a ruler had been born in Judea, so they went to Jerusalem, the capital city of Judea and the logical location of a king.

If they came from Babylon, they probably followed the same route that Abraham took from Ur to Canaan: going northeast along the Euphrates River, then south to Palestine through the Orontes River valley. A journey of about nine hundred miles.

THE JOURNEY

Let's imagine a cinematic depiction of their journey. Picture the Wise Men studying the stars night after night and consulting their enormous tomes to understand what they saw. One night, they observed a very unusual star. They exclaimed, "This must be the sign we've been waiting for! Certainly, this indicates the birth of the new ruler in Judah!" So they rushed around gathering gifts fit for a king, packing up necessary supplies, and tying everything to the backs of their camels.

(Cue soundtrack with low strings.) The picture fades to a night scene of three lonely men on camels crossing an empty desert.

Oops. Scratch that last scene. It turns out that we often think of three Magi because of the three gifts they brought Jesus: gold, frankincense, and myrrh. But in reality, the Wise Men's nine-hundred-mile journey to

Jerusalem needed a large caravan accompanied by servants and guards to protect the Magi and their precious cargo. So, keep the soundtrack but picture instead a crowd of people plodding through the desert with loads of supplies.

(Fade orchestra music. Replace with sounds of an ancient bustling city.) As the Magi entered Jerusalem, the people of the capital city gathered around this exotic-looking contingent. The Wise Men asked where they could find the new king. "We've seen His star in the east," they said, "and have come to worship Him." Imagine the looks on people's faces. Ordinary people didn't know anything about a new ruler.

(Cut to Herod's palace.) The notorious ruler paced as he ranted and raved. He had heard about the visitors arriving in the city. "A new ruler! What can this mean? Could these men from the East indicate that armies from that region will join forces with the Judeans to overthrow my government?"

Suddenly Herod stopped pacing and shouted, "Get the chief priests and scribes. Now!" When the religious leaders arrived, the distraught king asked, "Where is the Christ to be born?" They knew exactly where the Messiah would be born because it was prophesied in the Scriptures. "In Bethlehem," they told him.

Now that Herod had this information, he arranged a secret meeting with the Magi. As they entered his throne room, Herod ordered his men to close the doors. The men from the East drew closer to the throne, and Herod leaned in to ask, "So . . . when did you first see this star you've been talking about?" They recounted for him their heavenly observation and the journey across many miles.

(Cue evil sparkle in Herod's eye.) Herod told them to go to Bethlehem but to hurry back so that he could know the child's exact location and go worship Him.

(Orchestral music builds.) Can you see the Wise Men hurry out of the palace and into the night? (The music builds to a climax and then ends abruptly.) Even as the rest of the Magi rushed to the caravan, one man stopped and looked up at the night sky. Picture the joy on his face when he saw that the star had reappeared. He called to his companions and pointed to the amazing sight. They almost danced for joy as they quickly assembled their company and headed off to Bethlehem. Then the star actually moved, acting as their GPS for the last five to six miles to the stable where Jesus was born.

Oops. Scratch that. Take two. Matthew tells us that the star guided the Wise Men to a *house*. Although we often place the Wise Men at the manger in our nativity sets, they did not arrive on the night of Jesus' birth, or even the next day. By the time the Wise Men arrived in Bethlehem—which could have been as much as two years later—Mary and Joseph had found a house to live in. There, the Wise Men "saw the child with Mary His mother, and they fell down and worshiped Him" (2:11). Imagine the awe that was on their faces as the star stopped. They whispered, "This must be the place." They unpacked the treasures they had carried for nearly a thousand miles and reverently entered the house, kneeling to worship the young child. Eventually they got up and offered their presents—gifts fit for a king. Mission accomplished.

A JOURNEY TO WORSHIP

The map apps on our phones tell us how to get to our destinations and how long it will take to get to them. But the star informing and leading the Magi on their journey did one more thing: It told them why to go. The star signified that a new king had arrived! While it was customary for important people to honor and give gifts to new ruling dignitaries, the Wise Men made their arduous journey for an even greater purpose. They told the people of Jerusalem, "[We] have come to *worship* Him" (2:2, emphasis added). The theme of worship is present throughout this passage.

HEROD THE GREAT

The account of the Magi includes one villain: King Herod. He had a long reign in Judea from 37 BC to 4 BC.* The visit of the Magi frightened him because he knew he did not have a legitimate right to the throne since he was not from the royal line of David. He wasn't even a Jew. He was from Edom, the land of Esau's descendants. Herod obtained his position through his friendship with Marc Antony and retained his throne by pledging loyalty to the new Roman ruler, Octavius (Caesar Augustus), when Octavius defeated Antony.

Herod the Great was infamous for his ruthless behavior. He killed anyone suspected of plotting against him, including his brother-in-law, two of his sons, and his favorite wife. He discovered the accusations were false after the executions.

His paranoia over losing power led to the execution of the baby boys in Bethlehem. He asked the Magi to tell him when they saw the star announcing the arrival of the new King, and then he cruelly ordered the killing of all baby boys who could have been born since the star appeared. Based on the population of Bethlehem at the time, scholars estimate that about twenty boys were killed by Herod.

It is said that Herod ordered the arrest of many nobles near the end of his life, intending to have them slain on the day of his death to ensure mourning throughout the land. But when he died, the prisoners were released, setting off a great time of rejoicing instead.**

* *Some sources say 1 BC. Nevertheless, that Herod died in 1 BC or 4 BC does not indicate an error in Scripture but an attempt to adjust the calendar to reconcile ancient calendars, the solar year, and our modern calendar.*
** *See* NKJV Cultural Backgrounds Study Bible, *"Matthew 2:1: Herod the Great."*

Matthew contrasts the Magi's ardent desire to worship with the evil intentions of Herod. Yes, Herod told the Wise Men that he also wanted to worship the new King, Jesus, but we know what his true intentions were. He wanted to kill Him.

Although I'm not surprised by Herod's disdain for worshiping King Jesus, I'm astounded by the reaction of the chief priests and scribes. God appointed these people to lead the Israelites in worshiping Him and in anticipating the Messiah. Herod consulted them because they had studied the Scriptures and knew what they said about the Messiah. They had long awaited the fulfillment of the promise. So, at the news of a special star announcing the birth of the Messiah, I would expect them to jump up, pack their suitcases, and join the Magi on the last leg of their journey to worship the King.

But Scripture says nothing of their worship.

Scholars explain that the chief priests and teachers of the Law were part of the Sanhedrin, Jerusalem's ruling aristocracy. During this time, scheming Herod had reportedly killed members of the Sanhedrin who disagreed with him and replaced them with his own political supporters. So these chief priests and teachers who told Herod where the Christ would be born were perhaps afraid for their own lives or were possibly his constituents and more interested in retaining political clout than worshiping the one true God.

When I look at the difference between the Wise Men and the contingent in Jerusalem, I ask myself, "Who do I most resemble?"

- Am I like the Magi who traveled hundreds of miles to worship King Jesus? Do I share their exceedingly great joy at the opportunity to bow to the most important ruler?
- Am I more like Herod, who also wanted to find the King but did not want to worship Him? Am I like this notorious first-century BC ruler who only wanted to retain his own throne?
- Or do I act more like the religious leaders in Jerusalem who knew the Scriptures well enough to know who to worship but couldn't be bothered to travel a few miles to honor Him?

To be honest, my fallen nature pushes me to act more like Herod than the Magi. I don't want to give up my throne either. I would like to retain control of my own life, thank you very much. I also sometimes act like the priests and scribes, for I do know the Scriptures but I don't always go out of my way even a little bit to honor Jesus.

Matthew tells us that when the Wise Men finally found Jesus, "they fell down and worshiped Him" (v. 11). Throughout Matthew 2, the Greek word Matthew uses for *worship* is *proskuneo*. This word literally means "to fall upon the knees and touch the ground with the forehead as an expression of profound reverence." This form of adoration isn't very popular in today's culture because it points out our own insignificance in light of God's majesty. I might avoid this type of veneration because it acknowledges the following facts: Christ is great, and I am small. He is mighty, and I am not. He is King, and I am servant.

Modern society—which tells us to promote ourselves—would laugh at the thought of finding joy in humbling oneself. Yet when the Magi saw the star return after their encounter with Herod, they "rejoiced exceedingly with great joy" (v. 10). This short phrase has two words that mean joy and two words that mean great. They had mega *joy* in the prospect of bowing down and honoring this new King!

This kind of worship doesn't come naturally for me, but when I have bowed down to my Savior in adoration, I have found joy. As a baptized daughter of the King, **great, exceeding joy fills my heart when I truly praise my Father King because that is what I was created to do.** True worship takes the focus off me and puts it on the One who deserves all the applause. And when I worship, I am freed from the constant need to glorify myself.

THE STAR

For millennia, people have wondered about the star that guided the Magi. Some think it could have been an astronomical event. World history records such events around the birth of Christ. In 5 BC, Chinese and Korean astronomers recorded sighting a supernova. And on May 27, 7 BC, astronomers saw the conjunction of Saturn and Jupiter inside the constellation of Pisces. In ancient Babylon astrology, Jupiter represented the supreme deity, Saturn represented the Jews, and Pisces represented Palestine.

But most biblical scholars agree that since the star appeared, disappeared, then reappeared and moved, it was most likely a supernatural phenomenon.

GOD'S WORD AS OUR GUIDE

The Magi began their journey in the East because of a special star. In Jerusalem, the star reappeared and guided them to their destination. But in between, they needed help. Where did they obtain direction when they couldn't find their way? God's Word.

Herod certainly didn't have good intentions when he wanted to know the location of the Messiah, but he did know where to look. He asked the experts in God's Law. What did they say?

> They told him, "In Bethlehem of Judea, for so it is written by the prophet:
>
> "'And you, O Bethlehem, in the land of Judah,
> are by no means least among the rulers of Judah;
> for from you shall come a ruler
> who will shepherd my people Israel.'" (Matthew 2:5–6)

These religious officials knew their Scriptures and quoted the prophet Micah's words (see Micah 5:2).

We may not have a star to serve as our personal GPS, but we always have God's Word to guide us. I know, I know. Sometimes we would all like to have specific instructions like the Magi received. Even though you are an ardent student of the Bible, you probably haven't found a verse in Ephesians that tells you to marry Jim or a passage in Isaiah that says, "Take the job in Iowa." So instead of looking for specific directions, search Scripture for principles. What does it say about godly character traits in a spouse? What instruction does it offer about work and vocation? From those principles, we can assess our personal options and make God-pleasing choices.

Of course, knowing Scripture doesn't guarantee that we will pick the right action or choose the right road. Those religious leaders knew where to go but didn't follow through. We need to combine knowing God's Word with obeying God's Word.

Psalm 119:105 tells us, "Your word is a lamp to my feet and a light to my path." God's Word has the same function for us as the star had for the Magi. And just like the star went before them one mile at a time, God's Word often gives us just enough light for our next step. We would like to have the whole journey mapped out and explained. We would like the whole road ahead illuminated with LED streetlights. But the faithful lamp of God's Word shines a circle of light on the dark path, giving us guidance as we need it.

GO BACK ANOTHER WAY

Once in a while when I program my navigation system with my destination, the route it chooses makes no sense to me! As I make my way down the highway, it tells me to exit unexpectedly, and I wonder why. I decide that my way is better, so I ignore the directions and continue on the main highway. But a few miles down the road, all my smug feelings of choosing what I thought was the better route disappear when I discover that a horrendous accident has turned the interstate into a parking lot.

REMEMBER TO PACK: PERIPHERAL VISION

Should I sign up for this class? Or not? Should I quit my job? Or not? Often we see our choices as binary, focusing on a single decision with a yes or a no. We develop tunnel vision. But we increase our chance of long-term satisfaction when we use peripheral vision and search for additional options. Research shows that businesses that examined multiple options before making decisions rated those decisions as "very good" 40 percent of the time as opposed to a 6 percent satisfaction rate when only one option was considered.*

So, in addition to checking out that class, consider an online course or find books on the topic you want to learn more about. Instead of quitting your job, talk to your boss about your struggles or find a mentor in your workplace. Use peripheral vision and generate other possible options. Like the Magi, find another way.

"The Focusing Illusion: How It Distorts Your Daily Life," Wise Insights (website), accessed June 20, 2024, https://www.wiseinsights.net/focusing-illusion-distorts-daily-life.

The Magi had their route home all planned. They would go the way they came. Herod told them to go back through Jerusalem to tell him where to find the baby king. But God, like my GPS, changed their route in order to avoid danger. He told them in a dream to go back another way. They obeyed Him and avoided evil King Herod on their way home.

Sometimes in life I do exactly what I have done while driving. I sense that God's GPS is sending me a different way, but I have already made my plans. I have written my goals and plotted out my to-do list. Why change now?

Sometimes this happens in big ways, like when I've decided to tackle a new work project but begin to see that my concept won't work halfway through. But because I've made the goal and programmed the destination, I feel the need to complete it. I don't see the ten-car pileup ahead, so I keep going. But what if I became more open to letting the Holy Spirit lead and developed a willingness to change course?

Often my reluctance to alter my plans happens in smaller ways. In the morning, I may map out my day and construct a detailed task list. I manage to check off a couple tasks but then get an unexpected phone call. If I talk to this person, I know that the rest of my list will not get done—my day will take a detour. But even if my tasks do not get completed, perhaps talking with this person who needs a listening ear means I've followed God's plan for my day.

May I become more open to God's divine directions when He asks me to go back another way.

QUESTIONS FOR CLARITY

The Magi's journey to worship Jesus using God's star as a GPS gives us some principles to guide our lives. As we make decisions and formulate our plans, let's ask ourselves these questions:

- **How can I orient my life to worship Jesus?** Will taking the new job tempt me to worship worldly success instead of God? Or can I pursue this new position with an attitude of bringing glory to my Lord?
- **What principle in God's Word sheds light on my next step?** We may never find a passage that tells us to move to Tallahassee, but perhaps God's command to love our neighbor as ourself can help us decide to postpone a vacation and instead volunteer for a mission trip,
- **How has my stubbornness to achieve my own goals prevented me from listening to God when He wants to lead me in a better direction?** Think about times in your life when persistence in pursuing your own life objectives has not led you where you wanted to be. Looking back, can you see how God may have been telling you to go back a different way? What can you learn from that past experience?

DIVINE DIRECTIONS: LEAD US TO WORSHIP

When the Magi followed the star to see Jesus, the new King, it led them to an ordinary house. Jesus, the ruler of the universe, did not look like a king. He had no palace, no regal robes, no royal retinue. Yet they bowed down and worshiped Him because God had revealed to them that this ordinary-looking child was the King of kings.

Did you notice that the Bible doesn't say they bowed down to Herod? He certainly *looked* more like a royal ruler. Herod's home was a sumptuous palace with two main buildings, each with its own banquet halls and accommodations for hundreds of guests.[18] But the Wise Men worshiped the extraordinary child who lived in an ordinary home.

We can't see our King with our physical eyes today, so we may find it easier to orient our journeys toward things that look impressive: a fabulous home or a successful career. All the roads designed and constructed by the world lead to worship of self. They may have different names—Highway to Health, Road to Riches, or Skyway to Success—but they are all ultimately a dead end into a worship of what *I* want, desire, and crave. And although the world promises that making myself king of my life will bring me ultimate satisfaction, the destination is as disappointing as booking a trip to Cairo, Egypt, and landing in Cairo, Illinois. (No offense, Cairo, Illinois!)

Our broken hearts deceive us. So we struggle to believe that a life devoted to worshiping the King could satisfy and complete us. Yet that is exactly what happens.

When our lifelong journey takes us ever closer to worshiping the King, we have exceedingly great joy.

* * * * *

Lord, let my life be like the journey of the Magi:
oriented to worship You.
Let my pursuit of Your glory be my guiding star,
the GPS of my life,
the purpose of my journey.
Let Your Word
be a light to my path,
shine like a lamp on all my decisions,
show me my next step.
Let me be open to Your will even when it changes my plans,
interrupts my day,
doesn't look the way I expected it to.
And let this lifelong journey to worship You bring
great,
exceeding,
abundant
joy in You.
In Jesus' name. Amen.

PAUL

From Damascus Road to Gospel Highway

TIMELINE

Abram (Abraham)	ca. 2100 BC
Hagar	ca. 2081 BC
Rebekah	ca. 2026 BC
Moses and the exodus	1446 BC
Naomi and Ruth	ca. 1100 BC
Jonah	780 BC
The Magi	ca. 1–2 BC
Paul	ca. AD 6–68

My mother and I buckled our seat belts on the Southwest Airlines jet, grateful we had seats. My sister, who worked for the airline at the time, had sent both of us coupons entitling us to fly standby for free. I had flown internationally several times, so I knew firsthand the effects of delays and bad weather. But flying standby was a whole new adventure! Even if you make your way to the airport, find your gate, and show your standby pass to the gate attendant, you can never be sure you will make it on the flight. Paying customers and airline employees always have priority.

On this beautiful September day in 2014, my mother and I breathed sighs of relief as we settled into our seats. I texted my sister: "We're on the plane!" Soon we would be in Arizona to spend a few days with her.

The flight attendants went through their preflight procedures and announced that the doors had closed. We would now be pulling away from the Jetway and begin taxiing to the runway.

But the plane didn't move.

At first I wasn't concerned. At busy Midway Airport in Chicago, planes often wait their turn for a runway. But a few moments later, the pilot announced that the plane could not take off as planned because of a fire in the air traffic control facility in Aurora, Illinois (which, ironically, is only a few miles from my house). The crew didn't have much information at first, so we sat on the plane until it became clear it would not be going anywhere that day. My mother and I, along with all the other passengers, gathered our bags and went back into the terminal.

We waited in the airport for a couple of hours, hoping things would get resolved so we could catch another flight. But gradually we learned more about the situation.

The fire happened in the facility known as Chicago Center, which directed planes to and from Chicago and across the Midwest. A disgruntled FAA employee used his expertise to cut key wires and set a fire with gasoline-soaked rags. Everything in Chicago Center went dark, including radar and automated systems. Air traffic controllers could not direct planes in the crowded airspace over Chicago. They even had to evacuate the facility. Our flight was one of many from Chicago's O'Hare and Midway Airports that were grounded. Cross-country flights had to be rerouted over several states. The Aurora control center was offline for seventeen days.[19]

My mother and I never made it to Arizona that day, that week, that month. We had intended to visit my sister, but we were forced to cancel our plans.

Life is often like that. We make careful arrangements for our work, our families, our churches. But one person, one cut wire, one disaster can bring our plans to a screeching halt.

The life of the apostle Paul demonstrates how we can use our God-given gifts of intellect and wisdom to design wonderful itineraries for our lives. But we still need to adapt to God's plans when He clearly barricades a path we've chosen.

SETTING THE SCENE

Chapter 7 examined the Magi and their journey to worship the infant Jesus in about 2 BC. About thirty years later, Jesus fulfilled His earthly work "to seek and to save the lost" (Luke 19:10). Part of this work was to choose twelve disciples to learn from Him and then carry on the work of proclaiming the Gospel after He returned to heaven. The apostle Paul was not one of those twelve, but about three years after Jesus' death and resurrection, Paul (then known as Saul) met his Savior on the road to Damascus. Saul had intended to persecute and imprison the Christians in that city, but when he encountered a blinding light and the voice of Jesus, he was forever changed. Instead of "breathing threats and murder against the disciples of the Lord" (Acts 9:1), he became one of those disciples. He spent the rest of his life traveling approximately ten thousand miles to share the love of Christ.

THE JOURNEY

This is how I imagine the situation: "What was God up to?" Paul told Lydia he had asked himself this question a few weeks before he met her when he found himself on a ship crossing the Aegean Sea. Paul and his companions had not planned to come this way. They had intended to spend time in Asia Minor and Bithynia, but doors kept closing. Not sure where to go next, they traveled west to Troas, where Paul had a vision of a Macedonian man urgently pleading, "Come to Macedonia and help us." So they sailed one hundred fifty miles from Troas to the city of Neopolis in Macedonia. Then they journeyed from that port town to the important city of Philippi. When he arrived in Philippi, Paul could not follow his usual custom of speaking at a synagogue, so they walked out through the city gate to the riverbank, hoping to find a place of prayer.

And that's where Lydia met him.

Lydia and some of her friends had gathered by the peaceful river, an escape from the noise and hubbub of the city. When they saw a group of men walking toward them, they wondered what the men could want with them.

They addressed them kindly, and Lydia introduced herself: "I am Lydia. I live in Philippi." They showed genuine interest in the women, so she explained that she had originally come from Thyatira. There she learned how to dye clothing purple—a valuable skill in her day. She still made and sold purple goods.

As Paul started talking about God, Lydia assured him that she was a believer. But she had never heard the wonderful news he told her about Jesus. The more he spoke, the more the Lord opened Lydia's heart to hear and receive the Gospel. When Paul asked if anyone wanted to be baptized, she immediately said yes.

Lydia was moved to invite Paul and his companions to stay at her home while they were in the area. As they walked to her house, Paul told her the whole story of their journey to Philippi and how he had wondered, "What is God up to?"

Lydia believed that it was God's plan to lead Paul's ministry to her and her household so that they could be baptized. And she rejoiced that the Lord brought them to her!

TRAVELING COMPANIONS

As we already know, Paul logged about ten thousand miles on his journeys to preach the Gospel. If he could have earned points for miles of sea travel and number of steps taken, he would have been a platinum card member! In the book of Acts, the physician Luke recorded all of Paul's travels divided into three missionary journeys and a trip to Rome.

Paul's first missionary journey began in the city of Antioch in Syria. One day while the Christians there fasted and worshiped the Lord, "the

Holy Spirit said, 'Set apart for Me Barnabas and Saul for the work to which I have called them.' Then after fasting and praying they laid their hands on them and sent them off" (Acts 13:2–3).

Paul often traveled with a companion during his ministry. He understood the benefits of fellowship and teamwork. Having travel partners provided encouragement, protection, and opportunities for discipleship.

Encouragement. How appropriate that Barnabas was Paul's first traveling companion. Although his given name was Joseph, the apostles gave him the nickname Barnabas, which means "son of encouragement" (Acts 4:36). When Paul (then Saul) first attempted to join the disciples in Jerusalem after his conversion, you can imagine they might have doubted his sincerity! After all, they knew Saul as a Pharisee with a reputation for intense persecution of some of the first Christians. But Barnabas stood up for him and told the disciples how the Lord had spoken to Saul. As a natural encourager, Barnabas would have been a great blessing to Paul during his early missionary work.

On our own life journeys, God provides travel companions who believe in us, support us, and build us up along the way. At times, our ramble through life may get lonely. But the Lord gives us the blessing of brothers and sisters in Christ who strengthen us along the way. They might be our parents, other family members, teachers, friends, and pastors.

Discipleship. On Paul's second missionary journey, Paul met Timothy, who had probably become a Christian during Paul's first visit to Lystra. Timothy was the son of a devout Jewish mother, and he most likely had solid training in the Scriptures. By Paul's second visit, Timothy was "well spoken of by the brothers at Lystra and Iconium" (Acts 16:2), and Paul asked Timothy to accompany him on his travels. This gave Paul both another companion and the opportunity to disciple the next generation. As we move through life, let's also look for opportunities to pass on our faith and disciple those younger in age or younger in the faith.

Protection: During Paul's third missionary journey, he spent three months in Greece. When he planned to sail back to Syria from there, he discovered a plot against his life. To avoid this danger, he journeyed back to Philippi on foot. Acts 20:4 tells of some men who accompanied him and went ahead of him to ensure his safety.

We may not need people to guard us from death threats, but we may need someone to protect us from foolish choices. God will provide brothers and sisters in Christ to warn us of the cliff looming ahead of us when we can't see it. He will send a friend who can spot the danger to come when we might be tempted to choose a road that ends in disaster. **The Lord gives us the blessing of brothers and sisters in Christ who strengthen us along the way.**

FIRST MISSIONARY JOURNEY AD 47–48: PAUL'S ITINERARY

If you had traveled with Paul on his first missionary trip, you would have visited Selucia, Salamis, Paphos, Perga, Pisidian Antioch, Iconium, Lystra, Derbe, and Attalia. You would have sailed to some cities and walked many miles—perhaps twenty miles a day. In each city, you would have listened to Paul preach in local synagogues. In some of the cities, both Jews and Greeks (non-Jews) believed. But sometimes factions of Jews became jealous of Paul's popularity and stirred up dissension, forcing Paul and company to move on. Paul's first missionary journey took approximately two years and covered around 1,400 miles!

HOLY SPIRIT ROADBLOCKS AND REROUTES

How did Paul decide where to go? Did the Holy Spirit act as a travel agent and give him a daily itinerary? Not exactly.

It seems Paul used logic and common sense when he planned his trips most of the time. He followed the major roads and shipping lanes of his day. He visited major cities and cultural centers where the Gospel could have the greatest impact and reach. He visited cities with synagogues so he could first spread the Good News of Jesus to his fellow Jews.[20]

However, sometimes the Holy Spirit gave Paul specific travel instructions. During Paul's second missionary journey, the Spirit guided him in a surprising direction:

> And they went through the region of Phrygia and Galatia, having been forbidden by the Holy Spirit to speak the word in Asia. And when they had come up to Mysia, they attempted to go into Bithynia, but the Spirit of Jesus did not allow them. So, passing by Mysia, they went down to Troas. And a vision appeared to Paul in the night: a man of Macedonia was standing there, urging him and saying, "Come over to Macedonia and help us." And when Paul had seen the vision, immediately we sought to go on into Macedonia, concluding that God had called us to preach the gospel to them. (Acts 16:6–10)

Paul used his wisdom to plan his itinerary. He wanted to go to Asia Minor and Bithynia—both densely populated provinces of the Roman Empire. But in his attempts to go to both places, the Holy Spirit set up roadblocks. With routes barricaded to the south and north, Paul took the only option left: west.

When Paul came to the island of Troas, the Holy Spirit revealed Paul's next destination. This time we know the method: a vision of a Macedonian man asking Paul for help. Paul immediately set off once he knew which way to go.

What can we learn from this account?

Paul exhibited flexibility in following the Spirit's lead. Paul had made what seemed like wise choices for his next destinations, but when the Holy Spirit rerouted Paul to Macedonia, he went immediately. He didn't gripe and complain or try to argue the advantages of his travel plan. He obeyed without delay.

We can make plans, but we need to hold them loosely. When our plans to visit my sister were in jeopardy, my mother and I kept hanging on to the hope that flights would resume and we could still continue our trip. Eventually we had to face the reality that a journey to Arizona would not happen that day. In life, God sometimes similarly closes doors to what I have arranged. Do I accept the closed door and move on? Usually not. I often attempt to find a way around the blockade or strain to open the door on my own. However, this simply results in frustration. After my exasperation builds and nothing happens, I realize that my pride has prevented me from following God's lead. You see, pride insists that my way is best. But **humility acknowledges that God's wisdom exceeds my own**. Meekness and trust accept that the Lord's divine directions will always give me the most wonderful route for my life.

Following the Spirit may mean letting go of our own plans.

The Spirit revealed the course for his life. But how did this happen? A vision from God led him to Macedonia. However, that seems more of an exception than a rule in the guidance Paul received. When Paul was "forbidden by the Holy Spirit to speak the word in Asia," we don't know how the Holy Spirit communicated these travel diversions.

I've never received a vision like Paul did. I often wish the Holy Spirit acted like an air traffic controller. He has access to heavenly radar that can see the big picture of my life, thus clearly directing me exactly when to turn, when to pull up, and where to land. But He never seems to radio me with specific instructions. So how does the Spirit guide us today?

The Spirit primarily guides us through God's Word. Even when we think we have a strong impression that we feel is coming from the Lord, we need to make sure it aligns with Scripture. The Holy Spirit will not tell you to betray your spouse or cheat in your work because those activities clearly go against the Ten Commandments.

The Spirit can also work through wise Christian counsel. We can talk with a pastor, Christian counselors, and friends and relatives who exhibit faithfulness to God's ways to help us make wise decisions when we feel unsure about which way to go.

From Paul's example, we can see that God does not usually guide His people through extraordinary means. We can use logic and research to make wise decisions. We can follow the Spirit's lead as we spend time in God's Word, learn godly principles, and check all impressions and feelings against Scripture and Christian counsel.

SECOND MISSIONARY JOURNEY AD 49–52: PAUL'S ITINERARY

At the start of Paul's second missionary journey, a disagreement between Paul and Barnabas resulted in a parting of ways. However, Paul still valued companionship and chose Silas to travel with him. If you had accompanied them, you would have seen Paul's home province of Cilicia. Then you would have traveled to Derbe and Lystra, where young Timothy joined the traveling company.

Their itinerary took them to Phrygia, Galatia, Troas, Samothrace, Neopoplis, Philippi, Thessalonica, Athens, Corinth, Cenchrea, Ephesus, and back to Antioch. When you read that list, you probably recognize a few of the names. Paul established many of the churches he later wrote his epistles to during this missionary journey. He met Lydia, the "seller of purple goods" (Acts 16:14), experienced an earthquake that allowed him to be freed from prison (vv. 16–34), and preached his famous sermon about the "unknown God" in Athens (Acts 17:22–34) on this journey, which spanned about three years and 2,700 to 3,000 miles.

A SINGLE-MINDED LIFE

Paul's journeys teach us the value of traveling with companions and of following the leading of the Holy Spirit. But perhaps the most important lesson we can learn from his travels is his single-minded approach to life.

After avoiding the plot against him in Corinth, Paul doubled back to Philippi and set sail for Jerusalem as part of his third missionary journey. The ship stopped in Miletus on the way. While there, Paul sent for the elders of the church from nearby Ephesus. In a moving sermon to them, he clearly stated his life purpose:

> I do not account my life of any value nor as precious to myself, if only I may finish my course and the ministry that I received from the Lord Jesus, to testify to the gospel of the grace of God. (Acts 20:24)

From the time the disciples in Antioch first heard the Holy Spirit's call to set apart Barnabas and Paul to help spread the Gospel (see Acts 13:2), Paul lived out that calling. He dedicated his life to share the Good News of Jesus. Paul didn't travel to take in the sights, to pleasantly pass time with friends, or to collect frequent traveler points. He hiked over mountains and sailed on seas to tell the unbelievably Good News that no matter how much we have messed up (and Paul had been a murderous mess-up), Jesus' blood covers all our sin.

This mission of the Gospel influenced all his decisions. He went where people had not heard about Jesus. He traveled to strengthen the wobbly faith of new believers. He doubled back to churches where false teachers tried to pervert Jesus' Gospel. Paul's resolute commitment "to the gospel of the grace of God" (Acts 20:24) did not allow him to become sidetracked by hardship or tribulation. Angry Jews stoned Paul in Lystra and dragged him out of the city during his first missionary journey. They assumed he was dead. But when the believers came out to get his body, he got up and went with Barnabas to nearby Derbe the next day "encouraging them to continue in the faith" (Acts 14:22). Even imprisonment couldn't stop him on his second missionary journey. Paul witnessed to the jailer, and he and his whole family believed and were baptized (see Acts 16:33). Disciples at Tyre urged Paul not to go to Jerusalem at the end of his third missionary journey. They were certain he would face persecution. But Paul said, "I am ready not only to be imprisoned but even to die in Jerusalem for the name of the Lord Jesus" (Acts 21:13).

Whatever Paul did—whether preaching, teaching, traveling, or making tents to support himself so as not to be a burden to the churches—he wanted to spread the Good News of God's grace.

REMEMBER TO PACK: THE LORD'S PRAYER

One of my favorite spiritual practices is to slowly speak the words of the Lord's Prayer, pausing after each line to add my own words of praise and petition: "Our Father"—*Thank You for being a caring Father, one who watches over each step I take.* "Who art in heaven"—*I take comfort in knowing You can see my whole path from Your heavenly vantage point. You know every possible pothole, every bend in the road, every glorious mountaintop experience.*

Sometimes I spend my whole prayer time on the next phrase, "Hallowed be Thy name." Yes, we know that "God's name is certainly holy in itself, but we pray in this petition that it may be kept holy among us also."* I always pray that God's holiness and glory would be displayed in my little life, but I find this prayer especially helpful when I'm making decisions. I pray something like this: *Lord, hallowed by Thy name. Which of these choices glorifies You? Which one am I tempted to take because it brings me glory?* Often this prayer gives me the clarity I need, and I can move forward knowing the choice I have made does not conflict with my top priority: to love God wholeheartedly.

* *Small Catechism, The Lord's Prayer, First Petition.*

How would you describe your mission in life? And how does this single-minded purpose help you determine which paths to take and which roads to avoid?

Although we all have received the mission to "go therefore and make disciples of all nations, baptizing them in the name of the Father and of the Son and of the Holy Spirit" (Matthew 28:19), the way we each live out that mission will vary with our geographical location, season of life, and God-given talents and abilities. Paul lived out the mission through teaching and preaching, but we may follow Christ's directive through parenting, singing, teaching Vacation Bible School, or being an honest, hardworking employee.

I encourage you to craft a mission statement. Think about God's commands. Consider His values. Consider the talents and abilities the Creator gave you. Then write a statement specific enough to guide your decisions but general enough to take you through each season in life. (You will find more guidance in crafting a mission statement in the study guide for this chapter on page 200.)

My own mission statement is a work in progress, but it looks something like this:

> By God's grace, my mission is to love the Lord wholeheartedly and to love the people He places in my life. I will use my God-given gift of teaching to help others grow in faith.

During some seasons, this mission means I devote long hours to sitting at a computer to write a book. Sometimes it looks like traveling to retreats and workshops where I teach God's Word to sisters in Christ. But in some seasons, this mission statement guides me to say no to speaking and writing opportunities because I need to focus on loving the people God has placed in my life. When my husband's cancer returned, I wanted to be available to him during his six months of chemotherapy treatments.

When my daughter gave birth to baby number six, I directed my energy to helping her and her children.

A single-minded purpose reflecting God's priorities and our unique giftings will guide us through the twists and turns of life's decisions.

THIRD MISSIONARY JOURNEY AD 53–57: PAUL'S ITINERARY

If you had traveled with Paul, you would hardly have had time to do your laundry between the second and third missionary journeys. Acts 18:22 tells us that Paul concluded his second journey in Syrian Antioch. The very next verse says, "After spending some time there, he departed and went from one place to the next through the region of Galatia and Phrygia, strengthening all the disciples" (v. 23). You would have had the opportunity to unpack your suitcases for a bit on this journey. Paul spent more than two years in Ephesus, first preaching in the synagogues. Then he moved to the hall of Tyrannus when the Jews stubbornly refused to believe the Gospel. After a huge uproar among the silversmiths who were losing profits in their idol-making businesses, you would have left with Paul and company and traveled to Macedonia and Greece.

When Paul decided to sail back to Jerusalem, you and the rest of the disciples would have made stops in Troas, Asia, Cos, Rhodes, Patera, Tyre, and Ptolemais, finally landing in Caesarea. This third journey encompassed four to five years and about three thousand miles.

DIVINE DIRECTIONS: WITH FUEL FOR THE JOURNEY

Paul had wanted to go to Rome for many years. It was the largest city in the ancient Mediterranean world. In Paul's letter to the Romans, written around AD 55, he says, "I have longed for many years to come to you" (Romans 15:23). He finally made it to that metropolis of about one million residents around AD 57–58—but not as he had planned. Just as his friends had warned him at the end of his third journey, Paul was arrested in Jerusalem and, following a couple of years in custody in Caesarea, taken to Rome for his trial. He endured a shipwreck and a winter on the isle of Malta before finally arriving in Rome. Paul traveled about 2,300 miles during his trip.

He lived in Rome for two years under house arrest. But even in that less-than-desirable situation, Paul lived out his purpose to "advance the gospel" (Philippians 1:12) so that even the imperial guards knew his imprisonment was for Christ (see v. 13).

Luke ends the book of Acts with Paul still awaiting his trial.

> He lived there two whole years at his own expense, and welcomed all who came to him, proclaiming the kingdom of God and teaching about the Lord Jesus Christ with all boldness and without hindrance. (Acts 28:30–31)

Others traveled to Paul instead of him going to them. But the result was the same. Paul still preached the Gospel.

Was this the end of Paul's journey? Tradition says that Paul was released after two years of house arrest. Perhaps time ran out for the prosecutor's case. Some commentators think that the letter Paul wrote to the Philippians, composed while imprisoned in Rome, implies he would be released (see Philippians 1:19–26). Early Christian literature also mentions other journeys Paul took—perhaps as far as Spain. Paul's final journey took him back to Rome in AD 68, when Roman Emperor Nero ordered his execution (see the article "The Pauline Epistles" in *TLSB*). Paul lived out the words he penned to the Colossians no matter where he journeyed:

> We have not ceased to pray for you, asking that you may be filled with the knowledge of His will in all spiritual wisdom and understanding, so as to walk in a manner worthy of the Lord, fully pleasing to Him: bearing fruit in every

> good work and increasing in the knowledge of God; being strengthened with all power, according to His glorious might, for all endurance and patience with joy. (Colossians 1:9–11)

I feel convicted when I read this passage closely. Yes, I often ask God to give me His divine directions: "God, what do You want me to do? Where do You want me to go?" But what I really want to know is which path is the easiest path and which one will bring the most success. If I'm honest, my motives in seeking God's will are often self-focused.

QUESTIONS FOR CLARITY

Paul's extensive journeys give us instruction for our own life travels. Use these questions when you need to decide what your next step will be.

- **What travel companions has God provided for you?** Who can give you encouragement or protection as you journey through life? Who in your church or circle of acquaintances could you mentor or guide?
- **How can you use your God-given intellect and the Spirit's guidance when making decisions?** Will you use your mental power through research? Logic? Common sense? How can you remain open to taking the Holy Spirit's lead instead of holding on to your own plans? What specific steps can you take to search God's Word and seek Christian counsel?
- **What is your life mission?** What godly principles guide the direction of your life? How can creating a mission statement that considers God's purpose for your life and your God-given talents help you avoid wrong turns?

However, when Paul sought God's will, he didn't strive for a successful or comfortable life. He pursued the knowledge of God's will so he could please the Lord, know Him better, and bear fruit.

May we all travel through life like Paul, with a single-minded focus to glorify God and spread the Good News of Jesus. But friends, let's also remember that we are not on our own. We do not have to grit our teeth and hope that our own power will be enough to finish our trek through life. Because it isn't. Instead, we can be confident that **God will continually fuel our journeys with His glorious power—a miraculous strength giving us endurance that spills over into joy.**

* * * * *

O Divine Travel Guide,
what are You up to?
I thought You wanted me to take this path,
    travel this road.
But now,
    roadblocks bar the way ahead,
    barricades stand in the path I thought You had chosen.
O Lord, help me
    discover my next steps,
    find a new direction,
    determine Your itinerary.
I realize this may mean
    letting go of my carefully planned route,
    abandoning my desire for a comfortable
        and easy trip.
But more than anything, Lord,
    I want the beautiful path You
        have planned for me.
    I desire to live a life pleasing to You.
Give me the patience,
    endurance,

humility,
faith,
and strength
I need for my journey.
In Jesus' name. Amen.

EPILOGUE

At times I have silently called out, "God, would You please write in the sky exactly what You want me to do?"

You too?

Our hearts echo the cry of King David in Psalm 25:4: "Make me to know Your ways, O LORD; teach me Your paths."

I pray that as you have studied these accounts of how God led His people in the Bible, you have gleaned biblical principles that will guide your life. I have created an acronym with four steps we can use when we face a decision to help summarize what we have learned. As we journey through life, may we remember to take the TRIP with God.

> **T—Talk to God.** When considering various options, let's begin with prayer. But instead of simply praying for a clear sign in the sky, let us do the following:
>
> - **Pray for the willingness to obey.** Let's ask God to help us act like Abraham, who followed the Lord's command to go even when he didn't know exactly where God would lead him. Pray for the ability to say "I will go" like Rebekah.
> - **Ask for a teachable heart.** May we desire the humility that acknowledges God's ways are better than our own. Let's avoid Jonah's negative example of insisting on his own path. May we be willing to go back "by another way" and change course like the Magi.
> - **Pray for discernment.** Because we live in a Moab-like culture, pray for wisdom to distinguish between God's ways and the world's practices. Like Abraham, like Naomi and Ruth, let's willingly abandon an idolatrous road to follow a countercultural but godly path.
> - **Pray for faith and trust.** May we rely on God's steadfast love and faithfulness like Abraham's servant did, believing God always wants the best for us.

- **Ask for a single-minded purpose.** Let's ask God to help us define a life mission that, like Paul's calling, reflects the Lord's priorities and our God-given talents. May all our life journeys glorify God just as the Magi's journey to see King Jesus did.

R—Read God's Word. Although the Bible doesn't tell us to buy the house in the country or major in computer science, Scripture provides a road map for our lives. Seek out biblical principles and truths instead of looking for specific directions.

- **Look for the assurance of God's presence.** Even in wilderness times, He sees us just as He noticed Hagar.
- **Search out God's values and priorities.** Moses' journey included a stop at Mount Sinai where he received the Ten Commandments. The Ten Commandments and the rest of Scripture outline what God deems important. Even when we don't know *exactly* what to do, we can rest assured that we are in God's will when we obey God's commandments in His Word.
- **Read what the Bible says on the topic of your decision.** In the book of Acts, the Bereans diligently confirmed that Paul's words agreed with Scripture. When we face choices in our relationships, vocations, or anything else, we can also look to God's Word to read His views on the subject. The Bible won't say, "Marry Kevin," but it will give guidance on what to look for in a spouse.

I—Investigate Your Options. In addition to searching God's Word, explore other sources to help you make informed decisions.

- **Study and research your options.** In the book of Acts, it seems that Paul often used logic and common sense to determine where he would go. We can also use the amazing mind God gave us to research and obtain knowledge that will inform our decisions.

- **Investigate by consulting godly mentors and traveling companions.** Like Paul, we can surround ourselves with people who love the Lord and desire to do His will. When we need to determine which way to go, we can ask them for advice and guidance.
- **Use reflection.** The Angel of the Lord asked Hagar, "Where have you come from and where are you going?" Reflecting on how God has led us in the past or previously used our gifts can help us discern which road He is preparing us to take next.
- **Explore emotions.** Jonah allowed his anger to lead him in the opposite direction God wanted him to go. But our feelings can act as helpful signposts when we explore them with God. Why do you feel anger? Fear? Hope? Excitement? Let's ask God to help us make sense of our emotions through His Word.

P—Pick Something. After we've prayed, read God's Word, and investigated our options, we eventually need to make a decision. When we become overwhelmed by decision fatigue with the sheer number of possibilities or paralyzed by the fear that we will make the wrong choice, let's remember the following truths:

- **God will work everything out for our good.** He did that for Abraham when Lot chose the well-watered Jordan Valley and Abraham ended up with the seemingly second-best land. He did it for Naomi when He redeemed her bitter road. He did it by lovingly bringing back Jonah when the prophet purposely went the wrong way.
- **God will provide.** We can trust that God will give us everything we need when our life takes us straight into the wilderness, just like He did with Hagar.
- **God's road for our lives may resemble a zigzag path.** Moses didn't take a straight path on his way to becoming the leader of God's people. At times, all the options available to us seem small, insignificant, or even off-course. But God can use every twist and turn to send us exactly where He wants us to go.

- **God graciously bestows joy in the journey.** When we focus on God's presence in our lives, we can find contentment and delight along the way like Moses did, even if the road seems bumpy or dark.

When determining the course for your life or the direction of your very next step, remember that you are taking the TRIP of a lifetime with God. With every step you take, Talk to God, Read God's Word, Investigate Your Options, and Pick Something, knowing God works everything for your good. Rely on the Lord's divine directions.

* * * * *

Heavenly Father,
I want to follow Your path,
  walk Your road.
But at times I struggle to find that path,
  discover Your way.
Signposts along the road point in different directions,
  tempt me to walk on paths not meant for me.
So teach me Your ways.
  Open my ears to hear Your voice.
  Soften my heart to accept Your plan.
  Direct my eyes to see Your way.
  Guide my feet with the map of Your Word.
And as I travel on this road of life, remind me that
  Your constant presence accompanies me wherever I go,
  Your awesome power protects me in any storm,
  Your extravagant grace fuels every step.
Thank You for walking with me so that I can have joy in the journey.
In Jesus' name. Amen.

STUDY GUIDE

I invite you to learn more about how God leads us on our life journeys by going deeper into Scripture. You can read the accounts we've studied straight from God's Word and explore questions that will help you learn more about God's guidance. I have organized the questions in levels—not levels of difficulty, but levels of time.

Level 1: Reflect on the Reading: If you have only fifteen minutes, complete this section. These questions will help you reflect on the chapter's lessons and make them more personal. If you are doing the study in a group, these questions will get the conversation flowing.

Level 2: Dig into the Word: If you have more time, dive deeper in the Word by reading the Bible account of each journey and marking Scripture to help you glean more from the narrative.

Level 3: God's Word Is the Map to Your Life: Here you'll discover how to apply the lessons of each biblical journey to your everyday life.

Level 4: Create a Project: To help you internalize what you have learned, I have provided some practical exercises and hands-on activities. To encourage your heart, I've also included a playlist of music. You can find recordings of these songs on an online streaming service. If you are doing this study in a group, consider doing the activities together as people arrive for the session. The suggested songs could be playing in the background to create an atmosphere conducive to remembering God's gracious guidance. Perhaps one member of the group could take charge of getting materials for these projects and another of obtaining the playlist for the session.

To get the most out of this study, I encourage you to complete all the levels. But life is hectic. Do what you can!

CHAPTER 1: ABRAM: A TREK TO CANAAN

Reflect on the Reading

1. When you travel, do you have all the details of the trip planned out, or do you prefer to have the flexibility to make plans as you go? Why do you travel that way?

2. Imagine that God called out to you and said, "Leave your home. Go. I will let you know the route and destination along the way." How would you respond?

3. Do you often experience anxiety when you have a decision to make? How does Abram's account help you alleviate some of that fear?

4. What is your biggest takeaway from this chapter?

____

____

____

____

Dig into the Word

We discover new lessons when we carefully examine God's Word. One way we can do this involves looking for and marking specific words and phrases in the text. This week we will use this method with Genesis 12:1–9. You can mark your own Bible or mark the passage below. Look for the following details before you answer the questions.

1. Put triangles around all the names for God. What does this passage teach you about God and His character?

2. Circle the names of the people mentioned in this passage. What did you learn from their examples? Did they provide you with an example to follow or demonstrate a behavior to avoid?

3. Underline repeated words. What themes do these words show you?

4. Put a squiggly line under anything you found surprising. Why did this catch your attention? Did this create new questions that you want to investigate?

5. Put a box around the word you think is the key word of this passage. What is God teaching you about this topic right now? How does it apply to your journey?

Genesis 12:1–9

> Now the Lord said to Abram, "Go from your country and your kindred and your father's house to the land that I will show you. And I will make of you a great nation, and I will bless you and make your name great, so that you will be a blessing. I will bless those who bless you, and him who dishonors you I will curse, and in you all the families of the earth shall be blessed."
>
> So Abram went, as the Lord had told him, and Lot went with him. Abram was seventy-five years old when he departed from Haran. And Abram took Sarai his wife, and Lot his brother's son, and all their possessions that they had gathered, and the people that they had acquired in Haran, and they set out to go to the land of Canaan. When they came to the land of Canaan, Abram passed through the land to the place at Shechem, to the oak of Moreh. At that time the Canaanites were in the land. Then the Lord appeared to Abram and said, "To your offspring I will give this land." So he built there an altar to the Lord, who had appeared to him. From there he moved to the hill country on the east of Bethel and pitched his tent, with Bethel on the west and Ai on the east. And there he built an altar to the Lord and called upon the name of the Lord. And Abram journeyed on, still going toward the Negeb.

God's Word Is the Map to Your Life

When you use a physical map to chart your course, you take the following steps:

1. Determine your current location.

2. Pinpoint your destination.
3. Plot your course.
4. Follow the selected route.
5. Create checkpoints to avoid losing your way.

Let's use these steps to apply the account of Abram to our current situations and decisions.

Determine your current location. Where are you now? Describe your current situation. What decision do you need to make?

____

____

____

____

Pinpoint your destination. Think about what you hope to attain or feel when you have made this decision. (Remember that in nonmoral decisions, God may have many blessed options available to you.)

____

____

____

____

Plot your course. What principles from Abram's journey can guide you?

____

____

____

____

Follow the selected route. How can you apply these principles to your personal situation?

Create checkpoints to avoid losing your way. What Scriptures can act as signs to keep you on course? How can you keep them in view?

Create a Project

- In your journal or on a separate piece of paper, create a map of your life. Draw a simple map showing where you have lived. If you have moved a lot, this could be a map of countries, cities, or different homes within a city. If you haven't moved a lot, you could make a map of significant events in your life. Then, beside each place or event, write how God guided you and the faith lessons you learned at that place and time. Can you mark signposts where God's protective hand pulled you back from the brink of disaster, or where His grace redeemed you from disastrous wrong turns?

- Use music to remind yourself of God's gracious guidance in your walk of faith. Listen to "Guide Me, O Thou Great Redeemer" (*LSB* 918); "I'm But a Stranger Here" (*LSB* 748); "God Will Make a Way" by Don Moen; and "All the Way My Savior Leads Me" by Chris Tomlin.

CHAPTER 2:
HAGAR: ESCAPE INTO THE WILDERNESS

Reflect on the Reading

1. Have you ever been stranded on the side of the road? What happened and how did it make you feel?

2. Have you ever felt unseen? How does knowing *El-Roi*—"a God of seeing"—give you comfort?

3. In this chapter, we read, "When you cannot see a way forward in your journey, ask God to open your eyes to His provision." Have discouragement and disappointment ever acted as blinders, shielding your eyes from God's grace? Why does this sometimes happen? How can God open your eyes to His care?

4. What is your biggest takeaway from this chapter?

____

____

____

Dig into the Word

Let's mark specific words and phrases in Genesis 16:1–16. You can mark your own Bible or mark the passage below. Look for the following details before you answer the questions.

1. Put triangles around all the names for God. What does this passage teach you about God and His character?

2. Circle the names of the people mentioned in this passage. What did you learn from their examples? Did they provide you with an example to follow or demonstrate a behavior to avoid?

3. Underline repeated words. What themes do these words show you?

4. Put a squiggly line under anything you found surprising. Why did this catch your attention? Did this create new questions that you want to investigate?

5. Put a box around the word you think is the key word of this passage. What is God teaching you about this topic right now? How does it apply to your journey?

Genesis 16:1–16

Now Sarai, Abram's wife, had borne him no children. She had a female Egyptian servant whose name was Hagar. And Sarai said to Abram, "Behold now, the Lord has prevented me from bearing children. Go in to my servant; it may be that I shall obtain children by her." And Abram listened to the voice of Sarai. So, after Abram had lived ten years in the land of Canaan, Sarai, Abram's wife, took Hagar the Egyptian, her servant, and gave her to Abram her husband as a wife. And he went in to Hagar, and she conceived. And when she saw that she had conceived, she looked with contempt on her mistress. And Sarai said to Abram, "May the wrong done to me be on you! I gave my servant to your embrace, and when she saw that she had conceived, she looked on me with contempt. May the Lord judge between you and me!" But Abram said to Sarai, "Behold, your servant is in your power; do to her as you please." Then Sarai dealt harshly with her, and she fled from her.

The angel of the Lord found her by a spring of water in the wilderness, the spring on the way to Shur. And he said, "Hagar, servant of Sarai, where have you come from and where are you going?" She said, "I am fleeing from my mistress Sarai." The angel of the Lord said to her, "Return to your mistress and submit to her." The angel of the Lord also said to her, "I will surely multiply your offspring so that they cannot be numbered for multitude." And the angel of the Lord said to her,

"Behold, you are pregnant
  and shall bear a son.
You shall call his name Ishmael,

because the LORD has listened to your affliction.
He shall be a wild donkey of a man,
his hand against everyone
and everyone's hand against him,
and he shall dwell over against all his kinsmen."

So she called the name of the LORD who spoke to her, "You are a God of seeing," for she said, "Truly here I have seen him who looks after me." Therefore the well was called Beer-lahai-roi; it lies between Kadesh and Bered.

And Hagar bore Abram a son, and Abram called the name of his son, whom Hagar bore, Ishmael. Abram was eighty-six years old when Hagar bore Ishmael to Abram.

God's Word Is the Map to Your Life

1. When the Lord found Hagar in the desert, she named Him *El-Roi*—"a God of seeing" (Genesis 16:13).

   Psalm 32:8 also teaches us about this aspect of God. What does it say?

   ____

   ____

   ____

2. When you grasp the truth that God sees you and notices you, how does that help you when it feels like you're wandering in a wilderness all alone?

   ____

   ____

   ____

3. The Angel of the Lord asked Hagar, "Where have you come from and where are you going?" (v. 8). Pondering on your past can inform your future. Try my reflection practice. Consider the past thirty days by looking through your photos and calendar. Name activities and experiences that energized you and filled your soul.

   Now write about activities that left you feeling depleted and empty.

   While you can't always ditch unfulfilling tasks like cleaning the bathroom, knowing what refuels your soul and what drains you can help you make wise choices for future activities. Do you see any changes you want to make for the coming month as you look at your two lists?

4. Create a Project

- Try making a Middle Eastern dish like Hagar may have made for Abram and Sarai.

Hummus

Ingredients

1 (15-ounce) can chickpeas
¼ cup well-stirred tahini
2 tablespoons extra-virgin olive oil
Salt to taste
Dash ground paprika for serving
¼ cup fresh lemon juice
1 small garlic clove, minced
½ teaspoon ground cumin
2 to 3 tablespoons water

Directions

1. In the bowl of a food processor, combine the tahini and lemon juice and process for 1 minute. Scrape the sides and bottom of the bowl. Then process for 30 seconds more.
2. Add the olive oil, minced garlic, cumin, and a ½ teaspoon of salt to the whipped tahini and lemon juice. Process for 30 seconds, scrape the bowl, and then process for another 30 seconds or until well blended.
3. Add half of the chickpeas to the food processor and process for 1 minute. Scrape the sides and bottom of the bowl. Then add the remaining chickpeas and process until thick and relatively smooth, 1 to 2 minutes.

4. If the hummus is too thick and a bit lumpy, slowly add 2 to 3 tablespoons of cold water with the food processor turned on until you reach the perfect consistency.
5. Serve hummus with a drizzle of olive oil and a sprinkle of paprika.

- Praise God for being the God who sees you and opens your eyes to see Him. Some suggestions for songs to praise Him include "Be Thou My Vision"; "My Faith Looks Up to Thee" (*LSB* 702); "Open the Eyes of My Heart"; and "El-Shaddai."

CHAPTER 3: REBEKAH: A PATH TO A NEW LIFE

Reflect on the Reading

1. When have you had to say goodbye to something dear in order to move forward in your journey?

2. Do you feel the squeeze of culture? How much does the world's influence affect your decisions?

3. What is your reaction to the quote, "Following Jesus is not a three-week vacation. It's a lifelong expedition of saying, 'Yes, Jesus. I will go.'"

4. What is your biggest takeaway from this chapter?

Dig into the Word

We can discover new lessons when we carefully examine God's Word. We can do this by looking for and marking specific words and phrases in Genesis 24:34–67. You can mark your own Bible or mark the passage below. Look for the following details before you answer the questions.

1. Put triangles around all the names for God. What does this passage teach you about God and His character?

2. Circle the names of the people mentioned in this passage. What did you learn from their examples? Did they provide you with an example to follow or demonstrate a behavior to avoid?

3. Underline repeated words. What themes do these words show you?

4. Put a squiggly line under anything you found surprising. Why did this catch your attention? Did this create new questions that you want to investigate?

5. Put a box around the word you think is the key word of this passage. What is God teaching you about this topic right now? How does it apply to your journey?

Genesis 24:34–67

So he said, "I am Abraham's servant. The Lord has greatly blessed my master, and he has become great. He has given him flocks and herds, silver and gold, male servants and female servants, camels and donkeys. And Sarah my master's wife bore a son to my master when she was old, and to him he has given all that he has. My master made me swear, saying, 'You shall not take a wife for my son from the daughters of the Canaanites, in whose land I dwell, but you shall go to my father's house and to my clan and take a wife for my son.' I said to my master, 'Perhaps the woman will not follow me.' But he said to me, 'The LORD, before whom I have walked, will send His angel with you and prosper your way. You shall take a wife for my son from my clan and from my father's house. Then you will be free from my oath, when you come to my clan. And if they will not give her to you, you will be free from my oath.'

"I came today to the spring and said, 'O LORD, the God of my master Abraham, if now You are prospering the way that I go, behold, I am standing by the spring of water. Let the virgin who comes out to draw water, to whom I shall say, "Please give me a little water from your jar to drink," and who will say to me, "Drink, and I will draw for your camels also," let her be the woman whom the LORD has appointed for my master's son.'

"Before I had finished speaking in my heart, behold, Rebekah came out with her water jar on her shoulder, and she went down to the spring and drew water. I said to her, 'Please let me drink.' She quickly let down her jar from her shoulder and said, 'Drink, and I will give your camels drink also.' So I drank, and she gave the camels drink also. Then I asked her, 'Whose daughter are you?' She said, 'The daughter of Bethuel, Nahor's son, whom Milcah bore to him.' So I put the ring on her nose and the bracelets on her arms. Then I bowed my head and worshiped the LORD and blessed the LORD, the God of my master Abraham, who had led me by the right way to take the daughter of my master's kinsman for his son. Now then, if you are going to show steadfast love and faithfulness to my master, tell me; and if not, tell me, that I may turn to the right hand or to the left."

Then Laban and Bethuel answered and said, "The thing has come from the Lord; we cannot speak to you bad or good. Behold, Rebekah is before you; take her and go, and let her be the wife of your master's son, as the Lord has spoken."

When Abraham's servant heard their words, he bowed himself to the earth before the Lord. And the servant brought out jewelry of silver and of gold, and garments, and gave them to Rebekah. He also gave to her brother and to her mother costly ornaments. And he and the men who were with him ate and drank, and they spent the night there. When they arose in the morning, he said, "Send me away to my master." Her brother and her mother said, "Let the young woman remain with us a while, at least ten days; after that she may go." But he said to them, "Do not delay me, since the Lord has prospered my way. Send me away that I may go to my master." They said, "Let us call the young woman and ask her." And they called Rebekah and said to her, "Will you go with this man?" She said, "I will go." So they sent away Rebekah their sister and her nurse, and Abraham's servant and his men. And they blessed Rebekah and said to her,

"Our sister, may you become
  thousands of ten thousands,
and may your offspring possess
  the gate of those who hate him!"

Then Rebekah and her young women arose and rode on the camels and followed the man. Thus the servant took Rebekah and went his way.

Now Isaac had returned from Beer-lahai-roi and was dwelling in the Negeb. And Isaac went out to meditate in the field toward evening. And he lifted up his eyes and saw, and behold, there were camels coming. And Rebekah lifted up her eyes, and when she saw Isaac, she dismounted from the camel and said to the servant, "Who is that man, walking in the field to meet us?" The servant said, "It is my master." So she took her veil and covered herself. And the servant told Isaac all the things that he had done. Then Isaac brought her into the tent of Sarah his mother and took Rebekah, and she became his wife, and he loved her. So Isaac was comforted after his mother's death.

God's Word Is the Map to Your Life

1. Read Genesis 24:12–14 again and reexamine the principles we learned from Abraham's servant's prayer.

   a. **Begin your journey with prayer.** What do notice about the servant's attitude toward God? How does this match your thinking when you need to determine your next steps?

b. **Rely on God's steadfast love and faithfulness.** How does relying on these two qualities of God change the way you approach a decision?

c. **Respond in worship.** How can worship help even in the process of making a choice? Do you praise God when He answers a prayer?

d. Write a prayer using the three elements discussed above.

2. When Abraham's servant wanted to head back to Abraham and Isaac the very next day, Rebekah did not hesitate. She said, "I will go." Luke 9:57–62 tells about three men who expressed interest in following Jesus but then made excuses and didn't follow through. Read that passage and consider these questions.

   a. What excuses did the three men give?

   ____

   ____

   ____

   b. How do they contrast with Rebekah?

   ____

   ____

   ____

   c. When you need to make a decision and you think you have a God-pleasing option, do you immediately act or do you tend to make excuses and put it off? Why? Try to pinpoint emotions or mindsets that might make you hesitant to take action.

   ____

   ____

   ____

   ____

   d. How can Rebekah's story help you say, "I will go"?

   ____

   ____

   ____

   ____

Create a Project

- Examine the messages you receive from the world around you. Pay special attention to the values our culture communicates through commercials and media for one day. You might want to keep a notepad handy or use your phone's notes app to record what you discover. Then write some of those values in the space below. How do these standards compare to what God values? Does this exercise alert you to ways you might be influenced by the world?

____

____

____

____

- Reaffirm your willingness to say, "I will go," with these uplifting songs: "I Will Follow" by Chris Tomlin; "Follow You Anywhere" by Kristian Stanfill and Passion; "Let Us Ever Walk with Jesus" (*LSB* 685); "Lord, Take My Hand and Lead Me" (*LSB* 722).

CHAPTER 4: MOSES AND THE PEOPLE OF ISRAEL: EXODUS FROM SLAVERY

Reflect on the Reading

1. Have you ever experienced a detour or delay when traveling? How did you react? How did it affect your trip?

2. How can the long way sometimes be the best way when you travel and in life?

3. What values guide you through your life journey?

4. What is your biggest takeaway from this chapter?

Dig into the Word

Let's look for and mark specific words and phrases in Exodus 33:12–23—one of my favorite passages in all of Scripture. You can mark your own Bible or mark the passage below. Look for the following details before you answer the questions.

1. Put triangles around all the names for God. What does this passage teach you about God and His character?

2. Circle the names of the people mentioned in this passage. What did you learn from their examples? Did they provide you with an example to follow or demonstrate a behavior to avoid?

3. Underline repeated words. What themes do these words show you?

4. Put a squiggly line under anything you found surprising. Why did this catch your attention? Did this create new questions that you want to investigate?

5. Put a box around the word you think is the key word of this passage. What is God teaching you about this topic right now? How does it apply to your journey?

Exodus 33:12–23

Moses said to the Lord, "See, You say to me, 'Bring up this people,' but You have not let me know whom You will send with me. Yet You have said, 'I know you by name, and you have also found favor in My sight.' Now therefore, if I have found favor in Your sight, please show me now Your ways, that I may know You in order to find favor in Your sight. Consider too that this nation is Your people." And He said, "My presence will go with you, and I will give you rest." And he said to Him, "If Your presence will not go with me, do not bring us up from here. For how shall it be known that I have found favor in Your sight, I and Your people? Is it not in Your going with us, so that we are distinct, I and Your people, from every other people on the face of the earth?"

And the LORD said to Moses, "This very thing that you have spoken I will do, for you have found favor in My sight, and I know you by name." Moses said, "Please show me Your glory." And He said, "I will make all My goodness pass before you and will proclaim before you My name 'The LORD.' And I will be gracious to whom I will be gracious, and will show mercy on whom I will show mercy. But," He said, "you cannot see My face, for man shall not see Me and live." And the LORD said, "Behold, there is a place by Me where you shall stand on the rock, and while My glory passes by I will put you in a cleft of the rock, and I will cover you with My hand until I have passed by. Then I will take away My hand, and you shall see My back, but My face shall not be seen."

God's Word Is the Map to Your Life

1. Scripture talks about Moses' zigzag path to becoming the leader of the Israelites. Read about one of his detours in Exodus 2:11–25.

   a. Write about how Moses' life in Egypt might have contrasted with his life in Midian.

   ____

   ____

b. What do you think Moses learned during his time in Midian? How do you think this helped him become a leader?

c. Think about some of the zigzags in your life. What did God teach you when your path took an unexpected detour?

2. When God told the Israelites to turn and camp by the sea, they experienced terror as the Egyptian army approached them! Moses tried to calm their fears. Read his words in Exodus 14:13–14.

a. What did he tell the people to do? What did he say God would do?

b. Think of a situation in your life that brings fear or anxiety. Write how you can put Moses' instructions into practice by each phrase that follows.

Fear not: (Example: Instead of dwelling on my fears, I can turn to God every time I feel anxious.)

Stand firm:

See the salvation of the Lord:

Be silent:

Create a Project

- Use the spiritual practice of meditating on a Bible account. Find a quiet place and take time to calm your mind. Prayerfully read Exodus 14:15–31. Then close your eyes and picture yourself as one of the Israelites stepping onto that path through the Red Sea. What do you see? Hear? Smell? Feel? Taste? What emotions bubble up? Now imagine setting foot on the other side of the sea and seeing God defeat the Egyptian army. What goes through your mind as you witness this miracle? How does this strengthen your trust in God's ability to destroy the fears and enemies you currently face? Journal your thoughts and emotions below.

- Celebrate God's victory in Exodus and Christ's victory over sin and death in your life with music. Sing the hymns "I Will Sing unto the Lord" by Group Publishing and "Song of Moses and Israel" (*LSB* 925). Try listening to "No Longer Slaves" by Bethel Music or "Show Me Your Glory" by Third Day.

CHAPTER 5: NAOMI AND RUTH: A ROAD TO GRACE

Reflect on the Reading

1. When did someone help you find your way while you were traveling?

2. Ruth insisted on traveling with Naomi. How has having a companion helped you while traveling on trips? On spiritual journeys?

3. How does the account of God redeeming Naomi's bitter, painful road help you when you find yourself traveling on a path filled with obstacles?

4. What is your biggest takeaway from this chapter?

Dig into the Word

Let's mark specific words and phrases in Ruth 1. You can mark your own Bible or mark the passage below. Look for the following details before you answer the questions.

1. Put triangles around all the names for God. What does this passage teach you about God and His character?

2. Circle the names of the people mentioned in this passage. What did you learn from their examples? Did they provide you with an example to follow or demonstrate a behavior to avoid?

3. Underline repeated words. What themes do these words show you?

4. Put a squiggly line under anything you found surprising. Why did this catch your attention? Did this create new questions that you want to investigate?

5. Put a box around the word you think is the key word of this passage. What is God teaching you about this topic right now? How does it apply to your journey?

Ruth 1

In the days when the judges ruled there was a famine in the land, and a man of Bethlehem in Judah went to sojourn in the country of Moab, he and his wife and his two sons. The name of the man was Elimelech and the name of his wife Naomi, and the names of his two sons were Mahlon and Chilion. They were Ephrathites from Bethlehem in Judah. They went into the country of Moab and remained there. But Elimelech, the husband of Naomi, died, and she was left with her two sons. These took Moabite wives; the name of the one was Orpah and the name of the other Ruth. They lived there about ten years, and both Mahlon and Chilion died, so that the woman was left without her two sons and her husband.

Then she arose with her daughters-in-law to return from the country of Moab, for she had heard in the fields of Moab that the Lord had visited his people and given them food. So she set out from the place where she was with her two daughters-in-law, and they went on the way to return to the land of Judah. But Naomi said to her two daughters-in-law, "Go, return each of you to her mother's house. May the Lord deal kindly with you, as you have dealt with the dead and with me. The Lord grant that you may find rest, each of you in the house of her husband!" Then she kissed them, and they lifted up their voices and wept. And they said to her, "No, we will return with you to your people." But Naomi said, "Turn back, my daughters; why will you go with me? Have I yet sons in my womb that they may become your husbands? Turn back, my daughters; go your way, for I am too old to have a husband. If I should say I have hope, even if I should have a husband this night and should bear sons, would you therefore wait till they were grown? Would you therefore refrain from marrying? No, my daughters, for it is exceedingly bitter to me for your sake that the hand of the LORD has gone out against me." Then they lifted up their voices and wept again. And Orpah kissed her mother-in-law, but Ruth clung to her.

And she said, "See, your sister-in-law has gone back to her people and to her gods; return after your sister-in-law." But Ruth said, "Do not urge me to leave you or to return from following you. For where you go I will go, and where you lodge I will lodge. Your people shall be my people, and your God my God. Where you die I will die, and there will I be buried. May the LORD do so to me and more also if anything but death parts me from you." And when Naomi saw that she was determined to go with her, she said no more.

So the two of them went on until they came to Bethlehem. And when they came to Bethlehem, the whole town was stirred because of them. And the women said, "Is this Naomi?" She said to them, "Do not call me Naomi; call me Mara, for the Almighty has dealt very bitterly with me. I went away full, and the LORD has brought me back empty. Why call me Naomi, when the LORD has testified against me and the Almighty has brought calamity upon me?"

So Naomi returned, and Ruth the Moabite her daughter-in-law with her, who returned from the country of Moab. And they came to Bethlehem at the beginning of barley harvest.

God's Word Is the Map to Your Life

1. Read Ruth 2. Naomi and Ruth returned to Bethlehem at the beginning of the barley harvest.

   a. How do you see the providence of God working behind the scenes in this chapter?

   ____

   ____

   ____

   b. We often can't see how God will work everything out during our journeys. How does this account help you trust God in the unknown?

   ____

   ____

   ____

2. Read Ruth 4:13–17.

   a. What happy ending do you see here? How did the Lord redeem Naomi's bitter road?

   ____

   ____

   ____

   b. Now read Ruth 4:18–20. Why is this genealogy an additional happy ending for Naomi and Ruth—and us?

   ____

   ____

   ____

c. When have you seen God redeem broken roads in your life or others' lives?

---

d. Read Romans 8:28. How does this passage echo Naomi's story? Write a prayer expressing your trust in God's ability to work good out of pain.

Create a Project

- Ruth's words to Naomi in chapter 1 beautifully express love and loyalty. See the bookmark on the following page. Consider copying and coloring this rendering of Ruth's words and giving it to someone important in your life. Or you might keep it in your Bible to remind you to pray for the significant people in your path.

- Remember how God continually travels with us even on lonely roads through the hymns "Jesus, Lead Thou On" (*LSB* 718) and "Go, My Children, with My Blessing" (*LSB* 922). Revel in Jesus, your Kinsman-Redeemer, in the songs "Jesus, My Redeemer" by Christ Tomlin and "There Is a Redeemer" by Keith Green.

Image © IStock.com

CHAPTER 6: JONAH: DETOUR BEFORE DESTINATION

Reflect on the Reading

1. How do you react when weather or flight delays (or visits from presidents) force you to change your travel plans? Can you tell about a time when your plans were interrupted?

2. Have you ever purposely gone in the opposite direction when you knew God wanted you to go the other way? Or have you unintentionally made decisions that led you away from God for a time? Looking back, how did God orchestrate events to bring you back to Him?

3. Have you ever wondered if the book of Jonah is simply a parable? What did you learn from today's reading that supports it as historical fact?

4. What is your biggest takeaway from this chapter?

____

____

____

Dig into the Word

Let's mark specific words and phrases in Jonah 1. You can mark your own Bible or mark the passage below. Look for the following details before you answer the questions.

1. Put triangles around all the names for God. What does this passage teach you about God and His character?

2. Circle the names of the people mentioned in this passage. What did you learn from their examples? Did they provide you with an example to follow or demonstrate a behavior to avoid?

3. Underline repeated words. What themes do these words show you?

4. Put a squiggly line under anything you found surprising. Why did this catch your attention? Did this create new questions that you want to investigate?

5. Put a box around the word you think is the key word of this passage. What is God teaching you about this topic right now? How does it apply to your journey?

Jonah 1

Now the word of the Lord came to Jonah the son of Amittai, saying, "Arise, go to Nineveh, that great city, and call out against it, for their evil has come up before Me." But Jonah rose to flee to Tarshish from the presence of the Lord. He went down to Joppa and found a ship going to Tarshish. So he paid the fare and went down into it, to go with them to Tarshish, away from the presence of the Lord.

But the Lord hurled a great wind upon the sea, and there was a mighty tempest on the sea, so that the ship threatened to break up. Then the mariners were afraid, and each cried out to his god. And they hurled the cargo that was in the ship into the sea to lighten it for them. But Jonah had gone down into the inner part of the ship and had lain down and was fast asleep. So the captain came and said to him, "What do you mean, you sleeper? Arise, call out to your god! Perhaps the god will give a thought to us, that we may not perish."

And they said to one another, "Come, let us cast lots, that we may know on whose account this evil has come upon us." So they cast lots, and the lot fell on Jonah. Then they said to him, "Tell us on whose account this evil has come upon us. What is your occupation? And where do you come from? What is your country? And of what people are you?" And he said to them, "I am a Hebrew, and I fear the Lord, the God of heaven, who made the sea and the dry land." Then the men were exceedingly afraid and said to him, "What is this that you have done!" For the men knew that he was fleeing from the presence of the Lord, because he had told them.

> Then they said to him, "What shall we do to you, that the sea may quiet down for us?" For the sea grew more and more tempestuous. He said to them, "Pick me up and hurl me into the sea; then the sea will quiet down for you, for I know it is because of me that this great tempest has come upon you." Nevertheless, the men rowed hard to get back to dry land, but they could not, for the sea grew more and more tempestuous against them. Therefore they called out to the LORD, "O LORD, let us not perish for this man's life, and lay not on us innocent blood, for You, O LORD, have done as it pleased You." So they picked up Jonah and hurled him into the sea, and the sea ceased from its raging. Then the men feared the LORD exceedingly, and they offered a sacrifice to the LORD and made vows.
>
> And the LORD appointed a great fish to swallow up Jonah. And Jonah was in the belly of the fish three days and three nights.

God's Word Is the Map to Your Life

1. Jonah did not want God to interrupt his cushy life with an arduous journey.

   a. How do you respond when God interrupts your life plans? Can you think of times when this has happened in big and small ways?

   ____

   ____

   ____

   ____

b. Read Isaiah 55:6–9. What do you learn about God's ways compared to your ways?

c. How can these truths help you accept God's plans instead of insisting on your own plans?

2. Jonah's anger at the Assyrians affected his choices and his decision to obey God. Our emotions may also influence our decisions whether we are conscious of them or not. Take some time to examine your current emotions and record your thoughts below.

   a. Read Psalm 139:23–24. What do you notice about David's prayer?

b. Turn David's prayer into your own. Start with "Search me, O God, and know my heart! Try me and know my thoughts!" (v. 23). Help me sort out my messy emotions, Lord. Right now, I'm feeling . . .

____

____

____

____

c. Continue with, "And see if there be any grievous way in me" (v. 24a). Lord, show me if any of these feelings grieve You. Help me see if they contribute to wrong decisions or actions in my life. Right now, I see . . .

____

____

____

____

d. Finish with "And lead me in the way everlasting!" (v. 24b). Thank You, Lord, for never giving up on me. Even when my messy emotions lead me down the wrong path, You will bring me back to the "way everlasting." Right now, I'm grateful for . . .

____

____

____

____

Create a Project

- Read Jonah's prayer in Jonah 2. While in the belly of the great fish, Jonah called out to God. Write your own poetic prayer calling out to the Lord by following Jonah's example. Open up about your current troubles and thank God for hearing your prayers. End the prayer with Jonah's hopeful words: "Salvation belongs to the Lord!" (Jonah 2:9).

- Listen to music that reinforces the lessons of Jonah, such as "Jonah – Bible Songs for Kids" by DG Bible Songs on YouTube and "How Far" by Tasha Layton. Or sing "God Moves in a Mysterious Way" (*LSB* 765) or "I Leave All Things to God's Direction" (*LSB* 719).

CHAPTER 7:
THE MAGI: EXCURSION TO THE KING

Reflect on the Reading

1. When has using a map app helped you on a road trip? Has it ever led you the wrong way?

2. We hear the account of the Wise Men every Epiphany season. Did you discover anything new about them or their journey by reading this chapter?

3. Write about your reaction to this quote from the chapter: "When our lifelong journey takes us ever closer to worshiping the King, we have exceedingly great joy."

4. What is your biggest takeaway from this chapter?

____

____

____

____

Dig into the Word

Let's look for and mark specific words and phrases in Matthew 2:1–12. You can mark your own Bible or mark the passage below. Look for the following details before you answer the questions.

1. Put triangles around all the names for God. What does this passage teach you about God and His character?

2. Circle the names of the people mentioned in this passage. What did you learn from their examples? Did they provide you with an example to follow or demonstrate a behavior to avoid?

3. Underline repeated words. What themes do these words show you?

4. Put a squiggly line under anything you found surprising. Why did this catch your attention? Did this create new questions that you want to investigate?

5. Put a box around the word you think is the key word of this passage. What is God teaching you about this topic right now? How does it apply to your journey?

Matthew 2:1–12

Now after Jesus was born in Bethlehem of Judea in the days of Herod the king, behold, wise men from the east came to Jerusalem, saying, "Where is He who has been born king of the Jews? For we saw His star when it rose and have come to worship Him." When Herod the king heard this, he was troubled, and all Jerusalem with him; and assembling all the chief priests and scribes of the people, he inquired of them where the Christ was to be born. They told him, "In Bethlehem of Judea, for so it is written by the prophet:

"'And you, O Bethlehem, in the land of Judah,
  are by no means least among the rulers of Judah;
for from you shall come a ruler
  who will shepherd My people Israel.'"

Then Herod summoned the wise men secretly and ascertained from them what time the star had appeared. And he sent them to Bethlehem, saying, "Go and search diligently for the child, and when you have found Him, bring me word, that I too may come and worship Him." After listening to the king, they went on their way. And behold, the star that they had seen when it rose went before them until it came to rest over the place where the child was. When they saw the star, they rejoiced exceedingly with great joy. And going into the house, they saw the child with Mary His mother, and they fell down and worshiped Him. Then, opening their treasures, they offered Him gifts, gold and frankincense and myrrh. And being warned in a dream not to return to Herod, they departed to their own country by another way.

God's Word Is the Map to Your Life

1. God's Word is our guidebook for life. Although it doesn't give us specific instructions like "Buy the house on Twelfth Avenue" or "Major in social work," it contains the Lord's guiding principles for our journeys. Look up the following passages and write a biblical principle that could help you make decisions in the future.

   a. Psalm 1:1–3

   ____

   ____

   b. Proverbs 16:3

   ____

   ____

   c. Matthew 6:33

   ____

   ____

   d. Hebrews 13:5

   ____

   ____

2. Psalm 119:105 says, "Your word is a lamp to my feet and a light to my path."

   a. Read Psalm 119:130 and Proverbs 6:23. What do these verses say about God's Word as a light?

   ____

   ____

   ____

b. God's Word often acts more like a flashlight than a street-light. What is the difference between the two?

c. Think about a current decision and biblical principles that can act as a flashlight or lamp as you consider your next small step.

Create a Project

- The whole point of the Magi's journey was to worship King Jesus. Try one or more of these creative ways to worship this week.

  Worship through art: Create an artful rendition of this verse: "For we saw His star when it rose and have come to worship Him" (Matthew 2:2). Write it on a canvas, a note card, or in the margin of your Bible.

  Worship through words: Create an acrostic poem where each line begins with the letters of the word *King*.

  Worship through movement: Try singing praise to God while standing and raising your hands. Or use the *proskuneo* posture of the Wise Men, putting your face to the floor. (If you are unable to get on the floor, lie face down on your bed and worship.)

Worship through music: Immerse yourself in the lessons of the Wise Men through songs and hymns, such as "Christmas Offering" by Paul Baloche; "Emmanuel (Hallowed Manger Ground)" by Chris Tomlin; "As With Gladness Men of Old" (*LSB* 397); "The People That in Darkness Sat" (*LSB* 412).

CHAPTER 8: PAUL: FROM DAMASCUS ROAD TO GOSPEL HIGHWAY

Reflect on the Reading

1. When have extenuating circumstances forced you to cancel a trip? Did you learn any life lessons from that experience?

   ____

   ____

   ____

2. How have companions, family members, and friends provided encouragement, protection, or opportunities for discipleship in your journey through life?

   ____

   ____

   ____

3. In this chapter, we read, "Pride insists that my way is best. But humility acknowledges that God's wisdom exceeds my own." How have you seen pride interfere with your life as you try to follow the Spirit's lead?

   ____

   ____

   ____

4. What is your biggest takeaway from this chapter?

   ____

   ____

   ____

Dig into the Word

Let's mark specific words and phrases in Acts 16:1–15. You can mark your own Bible or mark the passage below. Look for the following details before you answer the questions.

1. Put triangles around all the names for God. What does this passage teach you about God and His character?

2. Circle the names of the people mentioned in this passage. What did you learn from their examples? Did they provide you with an example to follow or demonstrate a behavior to avoid?

3. Underline repeated words. What themes do these words show you?

4. Put a squiggly line under anything you found surprising. Why did this catch your attention? Did this create new questions that you want to investigate?

5. Put a box around the word you think is the key word of this passage. What is God teaching you about this topic right now? How does it apply to your journey?

Acts 16:1–15

Paul came also to Derbe and to Lystra. A disciple was there, named Timothy, the son of a Jewish woman who was a believer, but his father was a Greek. He was well spoken of by the brothers at Lystra and Iconium. Paul wanted Timothy to accompany him, and he took him and circumcised him because of the Jews who were in those places, for they all knew that his father was a Greek. As they went on their way through the cities, they delivered to them for observance the decisions that had been reached by the apostles and elders who were in Jerusalem. So the churches were strengthened in the faith, and they increased in numbers daily.

And they went through the region of Phrygia and Galatia, having been forbidden by the Holy Spirit to speak the word in Asia. And when they had come up to Mysia, they attempted to go into Bithynia, but the Spirit of Jesus did not allow them. So, passing by Mysia, they went down to Troas. And a vision appeared to Paul in the night: a man of Macedonia was standing there, urging him and saying, "Come over to Macedonia and help us." And when Paul had seen the vision, immediately we sought to go on into Macedonia, concluding that God had called us to preach the gospel to them.

So, setting sail from Troas, we made a direct voyage to Samothrace, and the following day to Neapolis, and from there to Philippi, which is a leading city of the district of Macedonia and a Roman colony. We remained in this city some days. And on the Sabbath day we went outside the gate to the riverside, where we supposed there was a place of prayer, and we sat down and spoke to the women who had come together. One who heard us was a woman named Lydia, from the city of Thyatira, a seller of purple goods, who was a worshiper of God. The Lord opened her heart to pay attention to what was said by Paul. And after she was baptized, and her household as well, she urged us, saying, "If you have judged me to be faithful to the Lord, come to my house and stay." And she prevailed upon us.

God's Word Is the Map to Your Life

1. Paul stopped in Berea during his second missionary journey. Read Luke's account of this visit in Acts 17:10–15.

   a. What did the Bereans do daily (v. 11)?

   b. How can this practice help us when discerning God's will?

   c. Luke says that the Jews in Berea "were more noble than those in Thessalonica" (v. 11). Scan Acts 17:1–9 to see what happened in that city. What did the Thessalonians do? What attitudes did they have that prevented them from accepting the Gospel?

   d. How do these same attitudes sometimes prevent us from discerning and accepting God's will for our lives?

2. We read how Paul's single-mindedness to preach the Gospel influenced all of his decisions in this chapter. Take some time to create your own mission statement that can serve as a guide for your future decisions.

   a. Start by reading Paul's mission statements in the following passages and answering a few questions.

      Acts 20:24: How would you define Paul's mission in life? How would you describe your overall mission?

      ____

      ____

      ____

      ____

      2 Timothy 1:11: What gifts did Paul have? What gifts and talents has God given you?

      ____

      ____

      ____

      ____

      Ephesians 3:7–8: What role did Paul say he had in this passage? How did he receive that position? Who did he minister to? Now consider what roles God has given you (think not only of your job but also of other roles in life such as daughter, mother, sister, and so on). Do you feel called to reach out to a particular group of people?

      ____

      ____

      ____

      ____

b. Taking into account the mission you have received from God, your current roles in life, and your particular gifts and talents, write a mission statement.

c. Like Paul, you have been given this mission in life "according to the gift of God's grace" (Ephesians 3:7). How does this change your perspective on your mission?

Create a Project

- Craft an artistic version of your mission statement using your own creative design. Or use the graphic below, writing your mission statement in the place provided and adding color. Consider putting a copy of your mission statement in your planner or posting it near your calendar to keep it visible as you make decisions on how to spend your time.

- Take some time to review what you have learned about God's guidance. Write some of the principles you want to take with you on your journey in the space below.

____

____

____

____

____

____

____

____

- Use music to remind yourself of God's mission for your life. Listen to "Thy Will" by Hillary Scott or "Nobody" by Casting Crowns. Sing "'Come, Follow Me,' the Savior Spake" (*LSB* 688) or "Hark, the Voice of Jesus Crying" (*LSB* 826).

PARTING THOUGHTS

In a world shouting, "Come this way!" or "Take these steps for success!" we often feel confused and overwhelmed. Which path should we take?

In *Divine Directions*, we have seen how God guides us through all the winding roads of life. The map of His Word leads us around each uncertain bend. His love accompanies us through every dark valley. But most of all, His grace leads us to our ultimate destination: eternal life with Him. Jesus clearly showed the road to heaven when He said, "I am the way, and the truth, and the life. No one comes to the Father except through Me" (John 14:6).

God's Word plainly outlines the path to Jesus and eternal life:

> *"For all have sinned and fall short of the glory of God"* (Romans 3:23). No one is perfect. Everyone fails to meet God's standard of sinlessness. This sin prevents us from coming to Him and from entering heaven.
>
> *"For God so loved the world, that He gave His only Son, that whoever believes in Him should not perish but have eternal life"* (John 3:16). God loved us so much that He sent His own Son to take the punishment we deserved for our sins and mistakes. Jesus' death enables us to live with God—forever.
>
> *"For by grace you have been saved through faith. And this is not your own doing; it is the gift of God"* (Ephesians 2:8). God gives us faith to believe in Jesus. His grace and mercy save us from death.

> *"But to all who did receive Him, who believed in His name, He gave the right to become children of God"* (John 1:12). By receiving Jesus in the waters of Baptism and the Holy Word of God, we become part of God's family.

I invite you to pray this prayer to the God who loves you and wants you to be part of His family:

> *Father in heaven, I realize that I am a sinner and fall short of what You want for my life. I know that I cannot save myself or earn eternal life. Thank You for sending Your Son, Jesus, to die for me. Through the power of His resurrection, You have made me alive eternally. Help me turn from my sins and follow You. Thank You for forgiving me because Jesus paid the price for my sins, even though I still fail. Thank You for Your gift of faith in Jesus, my Savior, and for the promise of eternal life with You. In Jesus' name I pray. Amen.*

God speaks His words of grace to you. Through God's free gift of faith in Jesus, you are part of God's family!

ACKNOWLEDGMENTS

Life is best when not traveled alone. I want to thank those who journeyed with me while writing this book.

John, thank you for the decades you've traveled with me through both joy and sorrow. I appreciate all the support, help, and humor you provide along the way. Thanks especially for reading all my words and offering helpful suggestions.

To my family: Anna, Nate, Aaron, Andrew, Alexander, Abigail, Attalia, Ariel, Nathaniel, and Mary—thank you for the delight and fun you add to my journey. Special thanks to Steven, Theresa, and Shelly for the marvelous voyage on the Hudson River when I desperately needed a break from writing.

To my writing friends Afton Rorvik and Michelle Diercks, who read drafts of the book and gave useful feedback.

To Rhonda, Sue, and Deb, who faithfully meet to study God's Word with me. Thank you for reading early chapters and helping shape this Bible study.

To Concordia Publishing House for believing in my writing once more. Special thanks to Peggy, Elizabeth, Erica, Anna, Laura, Tammy, and the rest of the team who help each book meet the needs of readers.

Above all, I thank the Lord for His guiding hand throughout my life and for giving me the privilege of sharing His Word with my sisters in Christ.

STUDY GUIDE ANSWERS

Chapter 1 *Reflect on the Reading:* Answers will vary.

Dig into the Word: Answers will vary but may include the following: *(1.) Names of God:* the Lord. When our English Bibles have "the LORD" written in small capital letters, it stands for the Hebrew word *Yahweh*, or *Jehovah*, God's covenant name. It means "the Self-Existent or Eternal One." This passage shows that God is a personal God, a God of blessing. *(2.) Names of the people mentioned in this passage:* Abram, Sarai, and Lot. These verses don't tell us much about Sarai or Lot, but Abram provides a positive example as one who obeyed God and set out in faith. God spoke to and appeared to Abram. *(3.) Repeated words: Blessing, Canaan, land, altar*, and many words related to travel such as *go, went, set out, passed through, moved*, and *journeyed*. God's blessing on Abram and blessing to the world through him provide a major theme for this passage and all of Abram's story. Canaan is the land of promise. The land is a key part of God's promise to Abram. Abram built altars to worship the one true God, demonstrating his faith in Yahweh. All the words related to travel demonstrate Abram's willingness to obediently go wherever God instructed him to go. *(4.) Something surprising:* One surprising thing is that God told Abram to go without even giving him a definite destination, and Abram obeyed Him. *(5.) Key word of this passage: Journey* and *blessing* are key words for this passage. Abram went on a journey out of obedience to God's call. God blessed Abram and blessed the world through him and his descendants, including Jesus. *God's Word Is the Map to Your Life:* Answers will vary.

Chapter 2 *Reflect on the Reading: (1.)* Answers will vary. *(2.)* Answers will vary. *(3.)* Satan will often try to discourage us and get us to forget God's love for us. But God's Word and fellowship with the Body of Christ can help us remember that God cares for us. He continues to work everything for our good (see Romans 8:28). *(4.)* Answers will vary according to the participants' experience. *Dig into the Word:* Answers will vary but may include the following: *(1.) Names of God:* "The LORD"—*Yahweh, Jehovah.* Angel of the Lord—appearance of the preincarnate Christ. God of seeing—*El-Roi.* This passage teaches us that Jesus was active throughout all human history. It demonstrates that God cares about all individuals—even those the world deems important and those the world ignores. It shows that God sees us even when we feel invisible. *(2.) Names of the people mentioned in this passage:* Abram was not perfect. He stepped out of God's guidelines for marriage and then allowed harsh treatment of Hagar. Sarai also does not give a positive example in this passage. She stepped in with her Plan B when she should have waited for God's timing. She dealt harshly with Hagar when Hagar conceived Ishmael. Hagar seemed to be the innocent one in the love triangle, but then she treated Sarai with contempt. Yet the example of God hearing her cries and blessing her with His presence gives us a picture of God's care for us. The name she gave God—"a God of seeing"—comforts us when we feel alone and invisible. *(3.) Repeated words: children, offspring, listened, seeing, looks after, fled, fleeing, conceived, pregnant, servant, mistress, name.* Not being able to have children is the start of many problems. Seeing is a major theme. Hagar's story informs us that God continually sees us and looks after our needs. *(4.) Something surprising:* One surprising thing is that the Angel of the Lord would appear to a foreign servant, to someone from a culture that didn't believe in the one true God. *(5.) Key word of this passage: Seeing* would be a good choice for the key word. God saw Hagar in the wilderness. Hagar saw the Angel of the Lord. She gave the Lord the name *El-Roi,* "a God of seeing." *God's Word Is the Map to Your Life: (1a.)* Psalm 32:8 says that God will teach us the way to go and guide as He keeps His eye on us. *(2.)* Answers will vary. *(3a., b., c.)* Answers will vary.

Chapter 3 *Reflect on the Reading:* Answers will vary. *Dig into the Word:* Answers will vary but may include the following: *(1.) Names of God:* "The LORD"—*Yahweh,* or *Jehovah,* God's covenant name. It means "the Self-Existent or Eternal One." God. The Hebrew is *Elohim,* a general name for God. But since it is the name for God used in the account of creation, it tells us that our God is powerful and mighty.[22] *(2.) Names of the people mentioned in this passage:* Abraham's servant provided a positive example of seeking God's guidance and worshiping Yahweh in thankfulness when his prayer was answered. The servant talked about Abraham's desire to not allow Isaac to conform to the pagan culture of the Canaanites. Rebekah is a positive example of trusting God's plan for her life and saying, "I will go." She was hard working and generous. The passage mentions Bethuel, Nahor, and Laban as relatives of Abraham. In Genesis 29, Laban's greed in his interaction with Jacob is shown, but we see hints of it in Genesis 24 when he runs to get Abraham's servant after seeing the rich gifts he gave Rebekah. In Genesis 24:63, we see Isaac meditating. This seems to paint him as a man of introspection and faith. He is also a positive example due to how he showed his love for Rebekah (and for Sarah, since he deeply mourned his mother's death). *(3.) Repeated words: wife, master, servant, send, worship, bowed down.* The whole passage talks about the Abraham's servant's search for a wife for Isaac. The master-servant relationship is an important theme because if we act like Abraham's servant, we will go where our Master directs us to go. *Send* is an important word because God often sends us on a specific road and asks us to respond, "I will go." The servant worshiped and bowed down in response to God's answers to his prayer. *(4.) Something surprising:* The fact that Rebekah agreed to go so quickly may be surprising. *(5.) Key word of this passage: Send* and *servant* would be good key words for this passage. Abraham sent his servant on a mission. God sends us on His missions. The servant displayed a powerful example of doing his master's bidding and relying on the God of promise. *God's Word Is the Map to Your Life:* Answers will vary.

Chapter 4 *Reflect on the Reading:* Answers will vary. *Dig into the Word:* Answers will vary but may include the following: *(1.) Names of God:* "The LORD," *Yahweh*, or *Jehovah*. We see in this passage that God is good, gracious, merciful, and so glorious that no man can look at His face. *(2.) Names of the people mentioned in this passage:* Moses. He yearned for God's presence and did not want to continue his journey if God would not go with him. His example of yearning for God's presence on the journey more than a specific destination is a good one to follow. *(3.) Repeated words: favor, presence, glory, gracious mercy, face.* The presence of God is an important theme because in the previous chapter, Exodus 32, God declared He would no longer go with the people of Israel. The glory of God is a theme throughout Exodus. Moses experienced the glory of God in ways no other human had. Moses found favor with God, which is also a significant theme. *(4.) Something surprising:* When Moses asked to see God's glory, God replied by saying He would make His goodness pass by. God's glory and character are essentially His goodness. *(5.) Key word of this passage: Favor* is repeated five times, making it the most repeated word in the passage. This could make it a key word because we know God's favor is not earned. Moses did not find favor because he was perfect but because of God's grace. We can also find favor with God because of Christ's saving work for us. *Presence* and *glory* would also be good key words for this passage because Moses desperately sought God's glory. Focusing on God's presence and glory in our own lives can transform our journeys. *God's Word Is the Map to Your Life: (1a.)* Possible answers: Moses probably lived in a large palace with servants to meet all his needs in Egypt. He probably lived in a tent in Midian. He needed to draw his own water. He was a lowly shepherd. *(1b.)* Moses probably learned humility. The best leaders do not place themselves above their followers. *(1c.)* Answers will vary. *(2a.)* Moses told the people to fear not, stand firm, watch for God's salvation, and be silent. He said that God would save them and fight for them. *(2b.)* Answers will vary.

Chapter 5 *Reflect on the Reading:* Answers will vary. *Dig into the Word:* Answers will vary but may include the following: *(1.) Names of God:* "the LORD," *Yahweh*, the covenant name for God. Naomi credited Yahweh for ending the famine in Judah and prayed for Yahweh to bless her daughters-in-law. Yahweh is a God of provision. Naomi also used the name *Almighty* (*Shaddai*), but she felt God's power had only brought her harm. However, the book of Ruth shows how the Almighty cares about our individual situations and can work all things for good. *(2.) Names of the people mentioned in this passage:* Elimelech, Naomi, Mahlon, Chilion,

Orpah, and Ruth. Elimelech took his family away from Israel and the worship of Yahweh. Some will say he exhibited a lack of trust in God's provision. Others will say that he used common sense in providing for his family. Naomi exhibited bitterness toward her circumstances and toward God. Given her sorrow, we can understand this. Her story shows us that God understands our sorrows. Following the example of many psalms, we can pour out our grief to God. Mahlon and Chilion took foreign wives, which was against God's laws. When we marry, we should find a spouse who shares our faith. However, God even redeemed their actions. Orpah did the logical thing and what Naomi urged her to do, but Ruth displayed the better example in willingly leaving her home country for a land that worshiped the one true God. Her example teaches us to have loyalty, love, and determination to follow the one true God no matter what. *(3.) Repeated words: return*, *bitter*, *die*, *wept*. The Hebrew word for return, *šûḇ*, appears twelve times as "return," "turn back," "gone back," and "brought me back" (Ruth 1:6, 7, 8, 10, 11, 12, twice in 15, 16, 21, twice in 22). Naomi returned to Bethlehem and experienced a spiritual returning to faith in Yahweh. But she was bitter. She told her daughters-in-law, "It is exceedingly bitter to me" (v. 13), and the women in Bethlehem, "Call me Mara [bitter], for the Almighty has dealt very bitterly with me" (v. 20). The Hebrew word for bitter is sometimes translated as "grieving." Naomi was bitter and grieving. The word *die* (or *died* or *dead*) appears five times (vv. 3, 5, 8, twice in 17). No wonder Naomi was grieving. There was so much death. The word *weep* appears twice, both times in the context of Naomi urging the younger women to go back to Moab (Ruth 1:9, 14). Their sorrow demonstrated the closeness they felt. *(4.) Something surprising:* If I didn't know the story so well, I would find Ruth's insistence to go to Bethlehem surprising. Leaving her birth family and culture would not have been easy. Her willingness to leave Moab demonstrated her desire to follow the one true God. *(5.) Key word of this passage: Return*, and its variations, is a good choice for a key word since it appears twelve times in this text. The word contains both geographical and spiritual significance. Naomi returned to her hometown. She returned to her God. The account of Naomi and Ruth urges all of us to repent and return to the loving arms of God over and over again. *God's Word Is the Map to Your Life: (1a.)* Ruth "happened to come to the part of the field belonging to Boaz, who was of the clan of Elimelech" (Ruth 2:3). Ruth didn't know which field to go to, but God led her straight to the field of the kinsman-redeemer. *(1b.)* Answers will vary. *(2a.)* Boaz married Ruth, and the Lord blessed them with a son who became Naomi's kinsman-redeemer. He would restore her life and nourish her in her old age (Ruth 4:15). *(2b.)* The genealogy shows that the child born to Boaz and Ruth would be the ancestor of King David, who would be the ancestor of Jesus, the Savior of the world, who gives salvation to all who believe in Him. *(2c.)* Answers will vary. *(2d.)* Romans 8:28 promises that God works everything for good for those who love Him. Other answers will vary.

Chapter 6 *Reflect on the Reading:* Answers will vary. *Dig into the Word:* Answers will vary but may include the following: *(1.) Names of God:* "Yahweh," the almighty God of covenant. Small *g* "god." The mariners called out to any god they thought could help them. "God of heaven." Here the Hebrew word for God is *Elohim*, "the Supreme God," "the creator of the sea and land." In this chapter, we see God as the controller of creation. We also see how He cares about people who do not yet know Him and how He works to bring His rebellious followers back to Him. *(2.) Names of the people mentioned in this passage:* Jonah and the mariners. Jonah provides a negative example in this passage because God gave Jonah a specific mission, and the prophet deliberately disobeyed Him. The mariners actually give a positive example because when they witnessed Yahweh's power, they feared Him and offered a sacrifice. *(3.) Repeated words: sea, ship, fear, afraid, lots, evil, flee, tempest, tempestuous.* The sea played a major role in Jonah's story. Fear is a significant theme in both the fear of the storm and the fear of the Lord. The lots could also be a theme of how God controls everything—even a game of chance. *Flee* is an important word because Jonah tried to run away from God. *(4.) Something surprising:* I find it surprising that Jonah was asleep while the storm was raging. *(5.) Key word of this passage:* Perhaps *fear* or *afraid* would be a good key word because of the fear of the storm. Also, Jonah described himself as someone who feared the Lord, but he did not demonstrate that respect with obedience. *God's Word Is the Map to Your Life: (1a.)* Answers will vary. *(1b.)* God's ways and thoughts are much higher than our own. *(1c.)* Answers will vary. *(2a.)* Answers will vary but might include David asked God to examine his thoughts and to search for anything displeasing to God. *(2b., c., d.)* Answers will vary.

Chapter 7 *Reflect on the Reading:* Answers will vary. *Dig into the Word:* Answers will vary but may include the following: *(1.) Names of God:* Jesus, King of the Jews, Shepherd, Christ. The name *Jesus* means "Jehovah is salvation." What a fitting name for our Savior! Jesus came as the King of the Jews but also the King of the world. Sending the non-Jewish Wise Men from the East to worship Jesus was one indication that Jesus came for everyone. The title *Shepherd* shows Jesus' nature as not an overbearing king but a gentle caretaker of our souls. *Christ* means the "'Anointed One,' who would deliver and rule God's people" (*TLSB*, "New Testament Names for God"). *(2.) Names of the people mentioned in this passage:* Herod, the king of Israel, and the Wise Men. Herod's evil example shows what happens when we refuse to worship the true King and instead try to retain the rule of our own lives. The Wise Men provide a positive example of willingness to journey to worship the ruler of the world. *(3.) Repeated words: Bethlehem, king, star, worship.* Jesus' birth in Bethlehem fulfilled the prophecy the prophet Micah spoke more than seven hundred years earlier. This shows how the Gospel winds through the entirety of the Bible. The repetition of the word *king* indicates a theme of this passage. What king do I worship? Do I bow down to the King of heaven and earth, or do I insist on being king of my own life? Worship is also a major theme. The Greek word can mean the reverence someone would show a king, but in the New Testament, it usually describes worship of the divine (see *TLSB*, note on Matthew 2:2). The star plays a major role in the account but also depicts Christ as the light of the world. *(4.) Something surprising:* Perhaps the most surprising thing is that the religious leaders who knew the Scriptures and waited and waited for the Savior didn't seem to follow the Magi to find Him. *(5.) Key word of this passage:* The words *king* or *worship* would be good choices for the key word. *God's Word Is the Map to Your Life: (1a.)* Seek out godly companions for life. *(1b.)* Involve God in every aspect of your life. Ask Him for wisdom. *(1c.)* Seek God first. *(1d.)* Guard against a love of money. Cultivate contentment because God is always with you. *(2a.)* Psalm 119:130 tells us that as the Holy Spirit unfolds God's Word to us, we gain understanding. Proverbs 6:23 teaches that even God's commands and discipline can shed light on our life paths. *(2b.)* A streetlight may light up a road, but a flashlight only illuminates a few steps ahead. God may not light up our whole life path, but He guides us step by step. *(2c.)* Answers will vary.

Chapter 8 *Reflect on the Reading:* Answers will vary. *Dig into the Word:* Answers will vary but may include the following: *(1.) Names of God:* "the Holy Spirit"—Third Person of the Trinity. "Spirit of Jesus"—another name for the Holy Spirit, who was sent by Jesus. "Lord" (not in small caps)—the Greek word is *kyrios*, meaning "master, supreme in authority." "God"—Greek word is *theos*, meaning "supreme divinity." *(2.) Names of the people mentioned in this passage:* Paul, Timothy, Lydia. Paul: a positive example of traveling to spread the Gospel. Timothy: a positive example as a believer and one willing to travel with Paul and serve Christ. Lydia: a positive example of one who hears the word and believes and also offers hospitality to Paul and his company. *(3.) Repeated words: went, women, woman, vision, faith, faithful.* Went: Paul and his companions went many places to tell people the Good News of Jesus. Women, woman: Paul did not discriminate against women but shared the Gospel with them too. Vision: Paul obeyed the Spirit when he received a vision urging him to go to Macedonia. Faith, faithful: Paul continually worked to strengthen the faith of the believers he encountered. *(4.) Something surprising:* It is surprising that God prevented Paul from going to Asia and Bithynia since they both had large populations where the Gospel could have had a big impact. We don't know why the Spirit blocked their way. *(5.) Key word of this passage: Went* would be a good key word for this passage. Paul continually went where God led him. The book of Acts shows Paul constantly on the move. *God's Word Is the Map to Your Life: (1a.)* The Bereans examined the Scriptures daily to see if Paul's words were correct. *(1b.)* Examining the Scriptures daily can help us learn God's values and priorities, which will help us make excellent choices for our lives. We can look to the Scriptures to see if there are commandments or principles that apply to specific decisions we are trying to make. *(1c.)* Some of the Jews believed, but others formed a mob and attacked Jason's house to find Paul. Their jealousy got in the way of accepting the Gospel because all they saw was Paul's popularity. *(1d.)* Jealousy can also interfere with accepting God's will for our lives. We might make decisions just to have what others have or to look good in the eyes of the world. *(2a.)* Acts 20:24: Paul's mission was to testify to the grace of God no matter what. 2 Timothy 1:11: Paul was a preacher, apostle, and teacher. Ephesians 3:7–8: Paul was given the role of minister through God's grace. He was called to minister to the Gentiles. *(2b.)* Answers will vary. *(2c.)* Answers might include the idea that because we have received our mission through God's grace, we realize it is not something we deserve or need to live up to. God's grace will also enable us to accomplish our mission.

ENDNOTES

1 See Howard S. Vos, *New Illustrated Manners and Customs: How the People of the Bible Really Lived* (Thomas Nelson, 1999), 6–18.
2 See Charles R. Swindoll, *Abraham: One Nomad's Amazing Journey of Faith* (Tyndale House Publishers, Inc., 2014), 21.
3 Sharla Fritz, *Waiting: A Bible Study on Patience, Hope, and Trust* (Concordia Publishing House, 2017), 13.
4 See R. Reed Lessing, *Deliver Us: God's Rescue Story in Exodus* (Concordia Publishing House, 2022), 19.
5 See Lessing, *Deliver Us*, 19.
6 See Lessing, *Deliver Us*, 119.
7 Lessing, *Deliver Us*, 264, emphasis in original.
8 See "Ruth and Naomi: Follow Their Path from Bethlehem to Moab on a Biblical Journey," Living Passages (website), accessed April 18, 2024, https://livingpassages.com/footsteps-ruth-and-naomi/.
9 See Liz Curtis Higgs, *The Girl's Still Got It: Take a Walk with Ruth and the God Who Rocked Her World* (WaterBrook Press, 2012), 16.
10 See Elizabeth Ahlman, *Ruth: More Than a Love Story* (Concordia Publishing House, 2014), 36.
11 Ahlman, *Ruth*, 47.
12 See Ahlman, *Ruth*, 73.
13 See Ahlman, *Ruth*, 135.
14 See *NKJV Cultural Backgrounds Study Bible*, note on Jonah 1:3.
15 See Priscilla Shirer, *Jonah: Navigating a Life Interrupted* (LifeWay Press, 2010), 28.
16 Because magic, necromancy, idolatrous astrology, enchantments, and syncretism were all forbidden in the Old Testament, I do not want to suggest that Daniel approved of any unbiblical practices. The prophet who braved the lions' den could not have incorporated sinful practices into his legacy at the school of prophets, which some commentators believe he established.
17 See R. C. H. Lenski, *The Interpretation of St. Matthew's Gospel* (Augsburg Publishing House, 1943), 68.
18 See "Herod's Palace," Bible History (website), accessed December 21, 2023, https://bible-history.com/jerusalem/herods-palace.
19 See "Controlled Chaos Heard During Aurora FAA Facility Fire," September 27, 2015, ABC 7 Eyewitness News (website) https://abc7chicago.com/brian-howard-aurora-fire-air-traffic-control-faa/1005524/ (accessed June 21, 2024).
20 See *Life Application Bible: New International Version*, (Tyndale House Publishers, Inc. and Zondervan Publishing House, 1991), note on Acts 28:16.
22 See Michelle Diercks, *Promised Rest: Finding Peace in God's Presence* (Concordia Publishing House, 2022), 20.

NOTES

NOTES